English coursework

Kevin Dowling has wide teaching experience in both the state and independent sectors and was most recently Director of Studies and Head of English at Bembridge School, Isle of Wight. He has been an examiner for the South Western Examinations Board, the Associated Examining Board, the Oxford Board and the Cambridge Board at CSE, O and A levels. He is the author of a number of Brodie's Notes including *Coriolanus*, *The War of the Worlds*, *Persuasion* and *A Farewell to Arms*.

GW00726936

Also available:

English coursework: **Conflict**
English coursework: **Prose**

Brodie's Notes on

English coursework

Drama and poetry

K. Dowling MA

Pan Books London, Sydney and Auckland

First published 1987 by Pan Books Ltd

This revised edition published 1991 by Pan Books Ltd,
Cavaye Place, London SW10 9PG

9 8 7 6 5 4 3 2 1

© Pan Books Ltd 1991

ISBN 0 330 50320 0

Photoset by Parker Typesetting Service, Leicester

Printed in England by Clays Ltd, St Ives plc

Drama and Poetry

Texts used in this book

Drama

Arden, *Serjeant Musgrave's Dance* 48
Bolt, *A Man for All Seasons* 48
Brecht, *The Caucasian Chalk Circle* 13–15, 22–7, 31–2, 40
Brighouse, *Hobson's Choice* 40, 48
Delaney, *A Taste of Honey* 48
Eliot, *Murder in the Cathedral* 40–1
Frisch, *The Fire Raisers* 48
Miller, *Death of a Salesman* 38, 48
Osborne, *Look Back in Anger* 48–9
Pinter, *The Caretaker* 49
Priestley, *An Inspector Calls* 39, 49
Rattigan, *The Winslow Boy* 42
Schwartz, *The Dragon* 49
Shakespeare, *Antony and Cleopatra* 37, 46–7
  Hamlet 37–8
  Julius Caesar 46–7, 49
  Macbeth 8–10, 39
  The Merchant of Venice 40, 49
  A Midsummer Night's Dream 32–3, 49–50
  Romeo and Juliet 10–13, 41–2
  Twelfth Night 41, 50
Shaw, *Androcles and the Lion* 50
  Arms and the Man 39–40
  Pygmalion 16–22, 33–4
Sheridan, *The Rivals* 41
Sherriff, *Journey's End* 41, 50
Stoppard, *The Real Inspector Hound* 42, 50
Thomas, *Under Milk Wood* 39, 50
Waterhouse, *Billy Liar* 28–31
Wilde, *The Importance of Being Earnest* 40, 42–6, 50

Poetry

Anonymous, *The Unquiet Grave* 87–8
  For Women 85
  The Blacksmiths 83–4
Blake, *The Clod and the Pebble* 82
  London 85–6
Frost, *The Road not Taken* 63–4
Hardy, *The Darkling Thrush* 57–60
  The Lodging-House Fuchsias 81
  Snow in the Suburbs 75–6
  Faintheart in a Railway Train 74–5
Heaney, *Death of a Naturalist* 55–7, 64, 73
Housman, *Is My Team Ploughing?* 88–9
Hughes, *Thistles* 60–2
Larkin, *Ambulances* 65–8
Owen, *The Send-Off* 84–5
  Anthem for Doomed Youth 68–70
  Dulce Et Decorum Est 71–3
  The Dead-Beat 76–8
Wilde, *Symphony in Yellow* 81–2
Wordsworth, *The Prelude* 86–7

See page 92 for the list of relevant Brodie's Notes on the above texts. These will help you with detail on your coursework and increase your knowledge of the book concerned.

Contents

Acknowledgements

The author and publishers wish to thank the following
publishers, authors and agents for permission to reprint
copyright material:

Jonathan Cape Ltd and the Estate of Robert Frost for 'The Road
not Taken' by Robert Frost from *The Poetry of Robert Frost* edited
by Edward Connery Lathem; Faber and Faber Ltd for 'Thistles'
by Ted Hughes, 'Death of a Naturalist' by Seamus Heaney and
'Ambulances' by Philip Larkin from *The Whitsun Weddings* by
Philip Larkin; Michael Joseph Ltd for an extract from *Billy Liar*
by Keith Waterhouse; The Society of Authors on behalf of the
Bernard Shaw Estate for an extract from *Pygmalion*; Methuen
London for an extract from *The Caucasian Chalk Circle* by
Bertholt Brecht and translated by James and Tania Stein and
W. H. Auden.

Preface by the general editor

The thematic approach to the study of literature has long been practised by teachers, and this new series of Brodie's Notes focuses on areas of investigation which will help teachers and students at GCSE and A-level alike.

The Notes will stimulate disciplined and imaginative involvement with your chosen books by widening your horizons to the possibility of studying works which are comparable in theme (say, Conflict) or genre (say, the Short Story).

Do not get so absorbed that you see *only* the theme under discussion and nothing else: the theme of any book – whether the presentation of marriage, or of love, or conflict – is only a part of the whole. Read primarily to enjoy and discover, and try to work out how important the theme you are examining is to the whole: it may reside in character or situation or social conditions or any number of areas. One thing is sure: by recognising and appreciating the theme or themes you will have learned more about the work you are studying. As a result you will be able to write about it more fully, and place it in a broader literary context.

The editor of each Theme/Genre Note in this series is an experienced teacher, and his or her aim is to promote your interest in a range of ideas and books – whether prose, drama or poetry, at the same time extending your capacity for literary appreciation and your imaginative participation in what you read.

For more specific help, you can refer to Brodie's Notes on individual texts.

Graham Handley 1991

Literary terms used in these Notes

ambiguity More than one meaning is suggested by the words. Consider the title of Wilfred Owen's poem, 'The Dead-Beat', where the implication is of exhaustion, defeat and death, almost a grim pun.

assonance A similarity of vowel sound within words that do not end with the same consonants.
e.g. made, mail, pain.

alliteration Words close to one another beginning with the same consonant sound, e.g. 'the swaying sound of the sea'. Look at the anonymous alliterative poem 'The Blacksmiths' (pp.83–4).

blank verse Unrhymed verse, usually referring to iambic pentameter (ten syllables having five strong beats). For example, the verse of many of Shakespeare's plays: 'How sweet the moonlight sleeps upon this bank!' See also, for example, Seamus Heaney's poem 'Death of a Naturalist' (p.55).

caesura An emphatic pause in the middle of a line of verse, and required by the flow of the verse – even though no punctuation is given.
'Swart, swarthy smiths [pause] besmattered with smoke
Drive me to death [pause] with the din of their dints.' (p.83).

diction The writer's choice of words. The particular vocabulary of the poem.
Compare, for example, the very different diction of the following poems:
'The Computer's First Christmas Card' Edwin Morgan
'Your Attention Please' Peter Porter
'An Elegy Written in a Country Churchyard' Thomas Gray

elision The omission of a vowel or syllable to make the words seem to melt together thus giving the verse greater fluidity.

epigram A witticism, sharp and concise, sometimes involving an apparent contradiction:
'Ignorance is like a delicate exotic fruit; touch it and the bloom is gone.'

euphemism Polite understatement. For example, describing 'death' as 'sleep'.

free verse There is no formal, regular pattern to the rhyme.

hyperbole Great exaggeration, not to be taken literally: 'Listen! I'm accused of war-mongering. Ridiculous! Am saying: ridiculous! Is that enough? If not, have lawyers along. About 500. Requisition all available seats for lawyers.' *The Caucasian Chalk Circle* Scene 5.

iambic pentameter The line of verse is made up of five 'feet', each consisting of two syllables, the first of which is stressed, and the second unstressed. Here is an example from the 'All the world's a stage' speech in Shakespeare's *As You Like It* (II, 7).

'And all the men and women merely players.
They have their exits and their entrances,
And one man in his time plays many parts,
His acts being seven ages. At first the infant,
Mewling and puking in the nurse's arms.
And then the whining school-boy with his satchel
And shining morning face, creeping like a snail
Unwillingly to school.'

imagery Mental pictures or sense-impressions conveyed by the expression of ideas or things in striking ways, usually by means of implied comparison:

'there's daggers in men's smiles'
'light thickens; and the crow
Makes wing to the rooky wood'
'After life's fitful fever he sleeps well' – *Macbeth*
'I have measured out my life with coffee spoons'
– *The Love Song of J. Alfred Prufrock* T. S. Eliot
'The force that through the green fuse drives the flower
Drives my green age' – Dylan Thomas

irony A deeper meaning derived from the opposite of what is stated literally.

'There's no art
To find the mind's construction in the face:
He was a gentleman on whom I built
An absolute trust.' – *Macbeth* (I, 5)

tragic irony A situation or a statement that has a significance unperceived at the time, and often where subsequent misfortune seems to mock the human condition.

dramatic irony Where the audience knows what a character or some characters on stage do not know, or where a character knows something that another character or characters don't know.

lyrical verse Poetry that is mainly concerned with the expression of the poet's thoughts and feelings. Read 'Hebrew Melodies' by Byron, for example.

metaphor A description of something in terms of something else without using 'like' or 'as'. A comparison that is implied within the line: 'This house has been far out at sea all night'. 'Wind' Ted Hughes.

metre When stress falls at regular intervals, 'metre' is the basic pattern of stressed and unstressed syllables. A combination of syllables, stressed and unstressed, is referred to as a metrical 'foot'. This part of a rhyme by S. T. Coleridge gives an indication of how technical terms can describe verse:

Metrical Feet
Trochee trips from long to short;
From long to long in solemn sort
Slow Spondee stalks; strong foot! yet ill able
Ever to come up with Dactyl trisyllable.
Iambics march from short to long; –
With a leap and a bound the swift Anapaests throng . . .

rhetoric The art of using words to persuade. See Mark Antony's speeches to the crowd in *Julius Caesar*, III, 2.

rhyme Identically pronounced consonants and vowels, usually at the end of a line. Partial rhyme is where there are subtle echoes of vowel sounds.

run-on lines Where the line of verse is not end-stopped by punctuation, and the reader is required by the sense of the poem to read beyond the line. By this means the verse frequently gathers rhetorical momentum.
'How many ages hence
Shall this our lofty scene be acted over
In states unborn and accents yet unknown.' *Julius Caesar*

satire A mocking wit that often distorts or exaggerates surface reality in order to emphasize an underlying truth. It exposes the follies and vices of society. See *The Importance of Being Earnest* Oscar Wilde, *The Real Inspector Hound* Tom Stoppard.

simile A means of comparison using 'like' or 'as', e.g. to fall 'like a stone'.

stanza Another name for a verse in a poem.

synonym A word that means the same or nearly the same as another word.

verbosity Wordiness. Using a great number of words when a few would be enough.

Introduction to coursework

This book is designed to assist students taking English or English Literature for GCSE by suggesting ways in which the compulsory coursework element of the examination may be approached. All the examples are constructed from poems and extracts from plays, and they may be used for either examination – although no one piece of work may be included in the coursework folders for both examinations. Obviously, a coursework folder for English – not English Literature – may also include writing (free composition such as poems, stories, plays of your own; examples of note-taking, summaries, letters) which is not based on literature, and which is not dealt with in this volume. However, it is worth emphasizing that the same reading material may be used both for coursework in English and in English Literature, and the assignments such as those illustrated in this book, will, when they are completed, be acceptable for inclusion in the coursework folder for either examination.

The term 'coursework' simply means any work undertaken during the course of study. This allows a wide interpretation; and while the assignments which follow reflect much of current and traditional practice in the teaching of literature, it should be remembered that no single list can ever be entirely comprehensive: there is an infinite range of approaches to the huge body of work that might generally be agreed to constitute 'literature'.

The principle behind the selection of extracts in prose and poetry is to provide the student with a model range which draws on established and contemporary literature. The treatment should be used as a guide for students using different material to that given here: the basic principles of approach will be the same and should be applied with discipline and imagination to *whatever* material you are using.

GCSE examinations provide for an element of coursework in all subjects; and, in English and English Literature, continuous assessment of the student's work during the course accounts for anything from 20% to 100% of marks awarded – depending on the particular syllabus, from whichever examining group of boards the school has chosen. Be sure that you are told the precise wording of your examination syllabus, so that you know exactly how many pieces of coursework you will need to include for final submission, of what variety they ought to be, of what length, and completed under what conditions.

The purpose of examination by means of coursework is to give you an opportunity to involve yourself more deeply in your work, so that you are not confined by time, or length of essay, or even by the efficiency of memory. The examination encourages the use of books during the completion of the coursework assignments – just as 'plain texts' or 'open book' examinations have allowed candidates to take set works into the examination room. The student is expected to comment in detail on the part of the text in question, and is not allowed to depend only on recall of the outline or of selected passages. Examination by this method can be an advantage to the dedicated and conscientious candidate, since it rewards genuine effort and appreciation. It gives you the time to read, think and write, and to rewrite, and so produce what is your best work. Your approach to coursework from the very beginning of the course, indicates how seriously you take the business of entering for a public examination.

A unit of coursework is normally expected to be about 400 words – two sides of A4 paper, approximately. Sometimes a longer piece may be included, for example if you are making an extended study of an author you are reading, or you are looking at several works which are linked in some way. Again, you must check this with the specific instructions in the particular syllabus you are doing. The file you keep will be made up of the many units you complete over the prescribed two years of the course. The best pieces will then be selected by your teacher and you for inclusion in the final examination folder.

The important things to demonstrate in your writing are:

KNOWLEDGE – of what you have been reading, what happens in the works and what they are about,

UNDERSTANDING – awareness not only of what is said plainly and literally, but of the deeper meaning that may be suggested or implied.

EVALUATION – which means coming to some conclusions yourself about what it is that makes the writing special, and being able to express what it has meant to you.

The more thorough your knowledge of the poems and plays (or extracts, if for English and not for English Literature), the greater will be your understanding; and the more searching and genuine your response and evaluation is likely to be. There is no substitute for getting to know the texts really well, by reading and re-reading them, by thinking and talking about them, by seeing the plays in performance and by performing in them, if possible, by reading what other writers have thought about them, and by writing about them for yourself. The suggestions in the following chapters indicate ways in which you can develop and express your 'knowledge, understanding and evaluation'.

It may help to know what the examiner is likely to be looking for. Any assignment you are set will be designed to allow for responses at different levels. A basic answer to a question about the importance of the first scene of *Macbeth*, for example, might say that in this scene three old hags meet on a bit of waste ground. A better answer might include the dramatic impact of an opening as mysterious and menacing as this, with its suggestions of darkness and the overturning of the natural order of things so that 'Fair is foul, and foul is fair'.

An indication of expected standards of achievement can be found in the GCSE 'grade descriptions' in the syllabus booklet for the examination you are taking. Grades A B and C are intended broadly to measure the standards set by the former 'O' level grades A B C and CSE grade 1; and grades D E F G to cover the standards measured by CSE grades 2, 3, 4 and 5. Generally, for grades A/B of coursework involving poetry and drama, you will be expected to demonstrate a high level of competence and to
– provide a full and complex treatment, particularly of texts chosen for close study, with reference to content, style and theme;
– undertake detailed analysis supported by references and apt quotations showing awareness of background within and across differences of author, genre, age, and culture;
– recognize and identify features of the writer's use of language such as imagery and structure, for example;
– recognize and discuss implicit as well as explicit meanings and attitudes within and across texts;
– convey a sensitive, perceptive, imaginative and informed response, clearly argued, with some evidence of originality, and sustaining personal as well as alternative interpretations;

– reach valid conclusions from comparisons made with other texts, and from wider reading;
– write with accuracy and control, in appropriately organized paragraphs, with careful choice of words and construction of sentences.

Very roughly, marks of 17–20 would indicate this level of attainment. However, this indication must be regarded with caution, since the recommendations of the examining groups differ slightly, and teachers may well prefer letter grades – particularly in the early stages of the course before final assessment has to be made. Do not regard the mark or grade during the course as a final assessment. The coursework marked by one teacher or centre has to be moderated (compared and adjusted) together with coursework from other centres (schools and colleges), and then re-examined by senior moderators and examiners before a final decision is reached. This is intended to reduce the element of subjectivity (personal judgement or preference with regard to content) in the initial marking, and to standardize the marks of candidates taught by different teachers in different centres.

For a C grade (marks 13–16/20) you will generally need to be able to:
– write in paragraphs, using sentences of varying complexity, taking care with spelling and punctuation;
– present material with clarity and accuracy;
– find relevant sections of the text to support your argument;
– give a general account of the text in your own words, and give detailed references and quotations when required;
– demonstrate awareness of themes, implications and attitudes in the writing;
– recognize and appreciate ways in which writers have used language and achieved particular effects (by the characterization and structure of a play, or the imagery of a poem, for example);
– communicate an informed and personal response (i.e. one based on knowledge and understanding, and not the product of instant reaction).

At a lower level, for grades F/G (1-8/20), candidates are generally expected to be able to:
– give an account of the poem or play in a straightforward way, identifying points of interest in plot or theme, (probably limited to repetition of narrative and situation);

– show some knowledge/insight/perception of the plays/poems
selected for detailed study;
– organize the material coherently, in appropriate paragraphs
for example;
– recognize obvious differences in style/way of writing;
– communicate some personal response, with reasons for this;
– describe the experience of reading the text, reflecting simply
on what it has meant;
– make limited comparisons with other material studied –
different texts by the same author, or on a similar theme,
perhaps;
– offer some reasoned judgement, for example of character and
motive.

The range of work in your file is important. Most literature
syllabuses require some poetry and some drama, with evidence
of wide reading beyond the basic or prescribed texts, and with
some evidence of an ability to make sense of poems and passages
from plays with which the student is not familiar. Examples of
each of these need to be available. The final examination coursework folder is a sample of the best work in your file, and since
the file containing all of your work provides your entry to part
or all of the examination, it is essential that the file is kept
carefully. Date all pieces, and keep a record sheet of the exact
assignment, the time that was allowed for the preparation and
completion of the assignment, the support that was available in
terms of teaching, group discussion, background reading, film/
video/broadcast/tape/performance, and the conditions under
which it was finally written up (at home or in the library, using
text and reference books as required, or in class, possibly under
test conditions). The presentation of the examination folder will
matter. Although we expect a piece of work to be judged according to its quality and not according to the attractiveness of its
presentation, nonetheless it is unrealistic to imagine that leg-
ibility, accuracy, and considered layout are not part of the process of communication. A good piece of work will be accurately
written and neatly presented. If the file is kept to a satisfactory
standard, the final selection will reflect this.

Drama

Drama: text and performance

In studying a play in depth you will have considered various aspects of it – plot, structure, setting, characters, dialogue, themes – and you will know something of the author's life and works as well as the general historical and social background that may be relevant. More important than all of this – you should see at least one production of the play, preferably on the stage rather than on film or video. The latter will help, as will records, tapes and broadcasts; but the unique vitality of a live performance is a product of the moment and cannot be recorded. You will gain insight from the experience, and this will bring the text alive. No one production can fully exploit the possibilities of a drama; so be alert to the peculiar nature of the production you see – for example, the decisions that have had to be made on the presentation of character, thematic emphasis, costuming, set design. Compare this with what your reading had led you to expect, and with what you may have seen on another occasion. Make notes recording your immediate impressions, and find out everything you can about the company and the production. Coursework that reflects the reality and excitement of dramatic performance will naturally be of a different calibre than writing which treats a play as if it were a novel abridged to dialogue. Try to keep fresh the immediacy of your experience of theatre.

When reading an extract from a play with which you are not familiar, slow down your reading and attempt to dramatize the scene in your own mind. You have to imagine and enter into the characters' feelings, hear the intonation of dialogue, listen for the pauses and the silences, see the movements, and watch facial expression. The script on the page is a bare outline of the drama that can be created; and your writing should reflect the fact that you can make something of the script for yourself. Practise reading between the lines to understand the emotions of the characters, and the tensions that may exist between them – recognize what is implied by the dialogue, as well as what is stated plainly.

Different modes of coursework assignment in drama

Here is a range of assignments suitable for inclusion in a GCSE coursework file for English or English Literature. The pattern reflects the move away from traditional essays towards a less rehearsed and more personal and imaginative response. The style of some of the 'open-ended' questions has received encouragement recently, but it may be judged by some teachers and examiners to have too little literary content to be satisfactory as coursework for English Literature GCSE. Caution in the framing of questions is advisable. Remember the importance of having a final folder of work that is balanced, and does not contain slight, trivial or experimental pieces at the expense of more substantial ones. Notes are provided in order to help the student appreciate the possibilities of the various forms of assignment which might be set. The examples discussed in detail are limited to particular writers so that the student is encouraged to read in support of the use of these notes. In this way the demands and the potential of some of the approaches to coursework may become clear.

Traditional structured questions

The questions within this type of exercise demand detailed knowledge and close reading, and tend to be of increasing difficulty. They frequently begin by focusing the student's attention on the meaning of particular words and phrases, gradually widening the range of interest to the implications of certain lines or speeches, inviting recognition and appreciation of features of style; and finally require a searching examination of aspects of the play – that is, comment supported by reference and quotation. Within the necessarily limited focus of the question, this means:

comment – observations on plot, structure, and characterization, presentation of principal ideas and themes, judgement/evaluation, personal response,

reference – referring in your own words to a word/phrase/line/ speech/feature so as to make clear what you mean by the above, and amplifying this by

quotation – selecting quotation to support/prove/illustrate, e.g. brief quotations in the flow of the sentence, longer

>quotations introduced by the sentence, and linking/
>explanatory comment.

A series of short answers to such questions will not normally be acceptable as coursework. The candidate is expected to offer evidence of study in depth: it is advisable to answer the questions fully, where appropriate. Indeed, it is perfectly possible to use the questions as a series of suggestions, or starting-points, for writing – allowing the questions to determine the paragraphing and provide the framework for a continuous composition.

The following assignment is an example of a traditional essay question for those who have studied a play in depth. Bearing in mind that GCSE literature syllabuses insist on an extended study of a complete work, the suggestions are generally applicable. *Macbeth* is a play which is common to many syllabuses, and, in any case, many students will have some experience of it. This assignment requires the organization of ideas and the marshalling of evidence, with some personal appreciation and response apparent from the way the scenes, characters, and language of the play are interpreted. The notes are designed particularly to illustrate the ways in which references and quotations can be used to support observation and comment.

Assignment

Macbeth is a play of darkness, blood and the unnatural. Is there any sense of the quality of goodness in the drama?

Notes

Consider the terms of the question. It begins with a statement of what the play is about. Do you agree that the dominant motifs – patterns – in the drama are created by 'darkness, blood and the unnatural'? Use your ideas on this to provide you with an introductory paragraph. You might refer to the darkness of the evil in the minds of Macbeth and Lady Macbeth, the mysterious symbolism of the witches and the heath, the horror of the 'direst cruelty' of the several murders, and the contagious corruption of a free country when men 'make good of bad, and friends of foes'.

The main thrust of your answer must obviously be prompted by the second sentence – the question of where in the play, if at all, there is created a sense of goodness, a natural world other than the world poisoned by the imagination and action of the central characters. Try to arrange your ideas so that the writing is based upon them rather than upon the sequence of the plot. You must avoid the convenient drift of the narrative – the 'Once upon a time there was a King ... and then ... and then' approach, plus an occasional reference to the topic. Jot down some ideas in rough, then re-arrange their order later, when you can see the whole pattern evolving. As you write, build up – in note-form at this stage – the supporting references and quotations that occur to you.

Look for references that refer to ideals of nobility, honour, courage, love, and to nature. 'Horrible imaginings' and 'the instruments of darkness' may dominate; but Macbeth has truly been 'valiant ... worthy ... noble'; Duncan is a virtuous king; Banquo and Macduff love their children; Lady Macduff and Young Siward symbolize the vulnerability of innocence and purity, and selflessness of heroism; and Malcolm knows that power usurped is barren and fruitless because authority proceeds from virtue:

. . .justice, verity, temperance, stableness,
Bounty, perseverance, mercy, lowliness,
Devotion, patience, courage, fortitude. (IV, 3)

Lady Macbeth has denied her humanity and destroyed herself. Macbeth is weary of the sun, and, without 'honour, love, obedience, troops of friends', can only look upon the future as a meaningless succession of tomorrows. The final scenes echo with a sense of irretrievable loss that testifies to what the dramatist regards as the indestructible nature of goodness.

One paragraph (half a page of A4, including in it references and quotations) could discuss the aspects of human nature that the play approves – even though these seem imperfect and overwhelmed. In other paragraphs you might examine the conduct of individuals of secondary as well as central importance. In conclusion, consider what you feel to be the most important and striking lines and speeches in the play, and see if you can find, running through all that is foul and false, allusions – often involuntary, perhaps – to reason, trust, the gentle senses, and to peace of mind.

Here are some examples of questions that might be set on a scene from *Romeo and Juliet*. The extract is part of III, 5 (see the *Arden* edition).

CAPULET: Hang thee young baggage, disobedient wretch!
I tell thee what – get thee to church a Thursday,
Or never after look me in the face.
Speak not, reply not, do not answer me.
My fingers itch Wife, we scarce thought us blest
That God had lent us but this only child;
But now I see this one is one too much,
And that we have a curse in having her.
Out on her, hilding.

NURSE: God in heaven bless her.
You are to blame, my lord, to rate her so.

CAPULET: And why, my Lady Wisdom? Hold your tongue,
Good Prudence! Smatter with your gossips, go.

NURSE: I speak no treason.

CAPULET: O God 'i' good e'en!

NURSE: May not one speak?

CAPULET: Peace, you mumbling fool!
Utter your gravity o'er a gossip's bowl,
For here we need it not.

LADY CAPULET: You are too hot.

CAPULET: God's breath, it makes me mad! Day, night, work, play,
Alone, in company, still my care hath been
To have her match'd. And having now provided
A gentleman of noble parentage,
Of fair demesnes, youthful and nobly lign'd,
Stuff'd, as they say, with honourable parts,
Proportion'd as one's thoughts would wish a man –
And then to have a wretched puling fool,
A whining mammet, in her fortune's tender,
To answer 'I'll not wed, I cannot love,
I am too young, I pray you pardon me!'
But, and you will not wed, I'll pardon you!
Graze where you will, you shall not house with me.

Look to't, think on't, I do not use to jest.
Thursday is near. Lay hand on heart. Advise.
And you be mine, I'll give you to my friend;
And you be not, hang! Beg! Starve! Die in the streets!
For by my soul, I'll ne'er acknowledge thee,
Nor what is mine shall never do thee good.
Trust to't, bethink you. I'll not be forsworn.

Assignment

1 What has made Capulet so angry?

2 What exactly does Juliet's father threaten her with?

3 What attitudes of Lady Capulet and the Nurse are apparent here?

4 Comment on the irony in Capulet's first speech.

5 How does Juliet respond to the various pressures that she comes under in the scene as a whole?

Notes

After the wedding night of her secret marriage to Romeo, Juliet has parted from her husband. He is now exiled from Verona because of his killing of Tybalt, Juliet's cousin, in revenge for the latter's killing of Mercutio, Romeo's friend. Juliet is told of the marriage her parents have arranged for her. She is to wed a worthy nobleman of the city. In tears, but determined, Juliet rejects this intention, although she cannot yet explain the whole truth behind her objection. Her father, old Capulet, takes Juliet's evident distress for ungrateful rebellion. He is furious that all his endeavours on behalf of his daughter should be scorned, as it seems to him, by a wilful girl. The angry father threatens the child. The mother coldly withdraws her love. Nurse, Juliet's companion, servant and friend, incites her charge to make the best of adverse circumstances by betraying her husband. Juliet can rely on herself only. Beset by sorrows, she is now harassed by her father's well-intentioned provision, her mother's chilly disregard, and the Nurse's practical amorality. Consider the predicament of the young girl. How do the events of the scene make Juliet more independent, and more mature?

Read the passage twice, to remind yourself of the scene. If you do not know the play well, read the whole of the scene. Remember that the questions should be used as starting points for your writing. Answer them clearly, but use reference and quotation to support your comments. Each question requires at least one paragraph of discussion. If you are not instructed to number your answers, then you may leave them simply as paragraphs which form the parts of a single composition. This is a way of allowing the set questions to provide you with the structure – or shape – of the piece of coursework.

Answer the first question by explaining that Capulet loves his daughter dearly, and he is exasperated that, now he has arranged for her to wed a man whom he considers an ideal choice, Juliet says she will not marry. You may refer back to I, 2, where Capulet talks to Paris about Juliet. The question tests your knowledge of what has happened earlier in the play and, in particular, what has happened earlier in the scene. You might quote lines that reveal Capulet's care for this daughter who is 'the hopeful lady of my earth', as well as some of those which illustrate his fury at being crossed in what he regards as action in Juliet's best interest:

Day, night, hour, tide, time, work, play,
Alone, in company, still my care hath been
To have her match'd.

Capulet threatens to disown and disinherit Juliet if she does not obey him. Try to point out the importance of lines like 'you shall not house with me' and 'what is mine shall never do thee good'.

Lady Capulet says practically nothing, which is interesting in itself; and Juliet's closest companion, Nurse, attempts to defend Juliet only to be overwhelmed by Capulet. Later, when Juliet turns to her nurse for consolation and advice, the Nurse recommends a deception that shocks the young girl:

I think you are happy in this second match,
For it excels your first.

Juliet must now act alone:

I'll go to the friar to know his remedy.
If all else fail, myself have power to die.

The question allows you to show that you are aware of Juliet's increasing independence and maturity.

Irony means an element of contradiction or double meaning (see p.xi) In the old man's first speech he calls Juliet 'a curse' and says that this only child is 'one too much'. We know that he is speaking like this because of his anger, incomprehension and frustration. Nevertheless, what he says in his fury does actually happen – a tragic irony and a terrible judgement on him.

The last question requires a detailed, planned examination of the whole scene. Consider the way her father, mother and her nurse try to influence Juliet. She has to withstand anger, ridicule, threats of various kinds, understandable but unjust accusations of ingratitude, emotional blackmail, and corrupt encouragement to betray her husband. Try to show where these pressures occur, and how Juliet's reactions develop during the scene.

Assignment

In *The Caucasian Chalk Circle* how does Grusha come to make herself responsible for Michael, and how does her sense of attachment grow?

Notes

The play was written at the end of the Second World War. Its author, Bertolt Brecht, was a German poet, singer and playwright who left Germany when Hitler came to power, and returned to East Germany after the war as director of the Berliner Ensemble theatre company. *The Caucasian Chalk Circle* reflects its author's communist sympathies, and its deliberately disjointed structure reflects his belief that an audience should not simply identify with the characters but should be made to think about their predicament, and the moral, social and political issues that give meaning to the drama and are given life by it. Brecht's anarchic energy and the warmth of his sympathy gives the play its charm. The message is relatively crude but patently sincere: the valley belongs to those who are good for it, just as the natural right of the foster mother takes precedence over the legal right of the mother who has abandoned her child.

The first scene is a discussion between members of two collective farms in the Caucasus (Russia). The conversation is what one might expect from a people with their history and recent trials. Now that the war is over, the 'Reconstruction Commission' will finally decide which group of peasants will continue to farm the land that has been devastated. The Expert is there to make the announcement. The Singer (narrator/commentator) is to entertain the villagers, and in doing so to guide them to an understanding of the wisdom of the play's principal idea – that what there is shall belong to those who are good for it.

The play opens up like a series of Chinese boxes. In Scene 2 the villagers become actors and dramatize the folk tale that they (we) are supposed to learn from. The setting is no longer contemporary. The action takes place in a feudal land of Princes, Ironshirts, a Grand Duke and his Governor, and peasants. The Governor of the province of Grusinia is overthrown by the power and ambition of the Princes, and in the chaos that follows his execution, the Governor's wife, Natella Abashvili, deserts their child. Grusha, a servant-girl, hesitantly and naïvely protects the child when the palace is threatened, and finds herself the only mother the infant has. Some time later, when a kind of order is restored, the Governor's wife tries to reclaim the child – although her motives are blatantly mercenary.

The play asks – and answers – the question: to whom does the child truly belong; to whom should he be given? The story derives from a judgement of King Solomon who is said to have decided such a case by offering to cut the disputed child in half, and awarding the child to the woman who proved her maternity by withdrawing her claim rather than see the child harmed.

The story of 'the Noble Child' is also 'the Story of the Judge'. A drunken village clerk, Azdak, by chance becomes the saviour of the fugitive Grand Duke and is later made a judge by marauding, villainous Ironshirts who are amused by the clerk's audacious, ironic wit. These are the soldiers (in the pay of the Princes), who have murdered the Grand Duke's Governor, and who cheerfully hang judges and beat carpet-weavers to a pulp. As fortunes turn, they are about to execute Azdak as an imposter when his 'appointment' is confirmed by a grateful, reinstated Grand Duke. The final judgement of the clerk is the case of the child, Michael, said to be son of the deceased Governor – and heir to his estate. The Governor's wife claims that a child who has been brought up by Grusha, formerly a palace kitchen-maid, is in fact her son, Michael. Azdak, with his garrulous wit, cynical view of formal 'justice', and his passion for a judgement that is based on truth and human needs, gives to Grusinia 'a brief Golden Age' that is 'almost just'. Grusha keeps her child, and is free to marry her soldier. The parallel is that the valley will go 'to the waterers, that it shall bear fruit'.

This assignment allows you to concentrate on plot and character. References are not difficult to find. Grusha is a simple hard-working girl who does not immediately understand the danger she places herself in when she adopts the forgotten infant – temporarily, she imagines. Try to explain the paradox of the singer's line, 'Terrible is the temptation to do good!' The merciful girl is chased by the merciless Ironshirts until, after she has attacked the Corporal and recovered Michael, 'the helpless girl became the mother of the helpless child'. Exploited by the peasants, and dependent on her own courage and self-sacrifice, Grusha protects the child by her 'marriage' with a 'dying' malingerer, only to be misunderstood by Simon, and in any case to have the child taken away from her. Consider the scenes that test Grusha, and the adversity that forges the link between the servant and the child-master, so that, when Grusha attends the court, what gives the scene its tension is the moral worth of her claim.

'Plain texts' questions

Here are examples of assignments that concentrate on a particular passage, whether or not the student is familiar with the rest of the play. The emphasis here is on the ability to discuss the detail of the extract. The 'open book' or 'plain texts' examinations that have encouraged this type of assignment have sought to reward the candidate who can make sense of the text when it is put in front of him, and who does not depend on recall or a rehearsed approach. The candidate's writing can be more spontaneous and creative, and a genuine response can be developed. The questions sometimes ask for commentary and appreciation:

commentary – this means going carefully through the passage, noting its dramatic effects, significances of plot development and of character,

of relationships, of
themes, and of the writer's intentions,

appreciation – how successful these prove to be,
and what your own reactions to the work are.

Sometimes the questions are deliberately directed, and your attention is focused on particular aspects of the passage – its importance in the play as a whole, for example, or the way in which it presents the shifting relationships of characters in the play. The expectation is that the argument you construct will be soundly based on what is presented to you, or on what you are asked to read.

Assignment

Read the extract (taken from Act II) of *Pygmalion* by George Bernard Shaw and write about the main ideas of the scene. What makes the exchange interesting and funny?

DOOLITTLE: Listen here, Governor. You and me is men of the world, ain't we?

HIGGINS: Oh! Men of the world, are we? You'd better go, Mrs Pearce.

MRS PEARCE: I think so, indeed, sir. *[She goes, with dignity]*.

PICKERING: The floor is yours, Mr Doolittle.

DOOLITTLE: *[to Pickering]* I thank you Governor. *[To Higgins, who takes refuge on the piano bench, a little overwhelmed by the proximity of his visitor, for Doolittle has a professional flavour of dust about him]*. Well, the truth is, I've taken a sort of fancy to you, Governor; and if you want the girl, I'm not so set on having her back home again but what I might be open to an arrangement. Regarded in the light of a young woman, she's a fine handsome girl. As a daughter she's not worth her keep; and so I tell you straight. All I ask is my rights as a father; and you're the last man alive to expect me to let her go for nothing; for I can see you're one of the straight sort, Governor. Well, what's a five-pound note to you? and what's Eliza to me? *[He turns to his chair and sits down judicially]*.

PICKERING: I think you ought to know, Doolittle, that Mr Higgins's intentions are entirely honourable.

DOOLITTLE: Course they are, Governor. If I thought they wasn't, I'd ask fifty.

HIGGINS [*revolted*]: Do you mean to say that you would sell your daughter for £50?

DOOLITTLE: Not in a general way I wouldn't; but to oblige a gentleman like you I'd do a good deal, I do assure you.

PICKERING: Have you no morals man?

DOOLITTLE [*unabashed*]: Can't afford them, Governor. Neither could you if you was as poor as me. Not that I mean any harm you know. But if Liza is going to have a bit out of this, why not me too?

HIGGINS [*troubled*]: I don't know what to do, Pickering. There can be no question that as a matter of morals it's a positive crime to give this chap a farthing. And yet I feel a sort of rough justice in his claim.

DOOLITTLE: That's it, Governor. That's all I say. A father's heart, as it were.

PICKERING: Well, I know the feeling; but really it seems hardly right —

DOOLITTLE: Don't say that, Governor. Don't look at it that way. What am I, Governors both? I ask you what am I? I'm one of the undeserving poor: that's what I am. Think of what that means to a man. It means that he's up agen middle class morality all the time. If there's anything going, and I put in for a bit of it, it's always the same story: 'You're undeserving; so you can't have it.' But my needs is as great as the most deserving widow's that ever got money out of six different charities in one week for the death of the same husband. I don't need less than a deserving man: I need more. I don't eat less hearty than him; and I drink a lot more. I want a bit of amusement, cause I'm a thinking man. I want cheerfulness and a song and a band when I feel low. Well, they charge me just the same for everything as they charge the deserving. What is middle class morality? Just an excuse for never giving me anything. Therefore, I ask you, as two gentlemen, not to play that game on me. I'm playing straight with you. I ain't pretending to be deserving. I'm undeserving; and I mean to go on being undeserving. I like it; and that's the truth. Will you take advantage of a man's nature to do him out of the price of his own daughter what he's brought up and fed and clothed by the sweat of his brow until she's growed big enough to be interesting to you two gentlemen? Is five pounds unreasonable? I put it to you; and I leave it to you.

HIGGINS [*rising, and going over to Pickering*]: Pickering: if we were to take this man in hand for three months, he could choose between a seat in the Cabinet and a popular pulpit in Wales.

PICKERING: What do you say to that, Doolittle?

DOOLITTLE: Not me, Governor, thank you kindly. I've heard all the preachers and all the prime ministers – for I'm a thinking man and game for politics or religion or social reform same as all the other amusements – and I tell you it's a dog's life any way you look at it. Undeserving poverty is my line. Taking one station in society with another, it's – it's – well, it's the only one that has any ginger in it, to my taste.

HIGGINS: I suppose we must give him a fiver.

PICKERING: He'll make bad use of it, I'm afraid.

DOOLITTLE: Not me, Governor, so help me I won't. Don't you be afraid that I'll save it and spare it and live idle on it. There won't be a penny of it left by Monday: I'll have to go to work same as if I'd never had it. It won't pauperize me, you bet. Just one good spree for myself and the missus, giving pleasure to ourselves and employment to others, and satisfaction to you to think it's not been throwed away. You couldn't spend it better.

HIGGINS [taking out his pocket book and coming between Doolittle and the piano]: This is irresistible. Let's give him ten. [He offers two notes to the dustman].

DOOLITTLE: No, Governor. She wouldn't have the heart to spend ten; and perhaps I shouldn't neither. Ten pounds is a lot of money: it makes a man feel prudent like; and then good-bye to happiness. You give me what I ask you, Governor: not a penny more, and not a penny less.

PICKERING: Why don't you marry that missus of yours? I rather draw the line at encouraging that kind of immorality.

DOOLITTLE: Tell her so, Governor; tell her so. I'm willing. It's me that suffers by it. I've no hold on her. I got to be agreeable to her. I got to give her presents. I got to buy her clothes something sinful. I'm a slave to that woman, Governor, just because I'm not her lawful husband. And she knows it too. Catch her marrying me! Take my advice, Governor – marry Eliza while she's young and don't know no better. If you don't you'll be sorry for it after. If you do she'll be sorry for it after; but better her than you, because you're a man and she's only a woman and don't know how to be happy anyhow.

HIGGINS: Pickering: If we listen to this man another minute, we shall have no convictions left. [To Doolittle] Five pounds I think you said.

Notes

This is a witty, satirical play. George Bernard Shaw was a drama-tist of ideas rather than of personalities and relationships, and his work is a criticism of society. The comedy is mainly verbal. It is produced by the sharp epigrammatic way the characters say what they have to say in their situations. What the characters do and what happens to them is important of course, but is not at the heart of the comedy. The characters are really figures designed to present ideas in stimulating and thought-provoking ways. They are not real people with whose fates it is tempting to identify. Comedy is a way of looking at life, and perhaps a means of coming to terms with it. It is a positive admission of absurdity, inadequacy and self-deception and of the odd dignity inherent in the refusal to give up the uneven struggle against the combined odds of fate and human nature. Shaw's humour is a paradoxical twisting of the knife. He shows the audience what they are by making his characters say, in an exaggerated form, what the audience actually thinks – although it may not either know or admit this. The target of Shaw's satirical humour is the audience, not the characters. The universality of comedy lies in the generalizations made in a play about the way people behave and the motives they ascribe to their conduct. Any play with a satirical vein will distort the normal 'real' appearance of things in order to highlight an underlying condition which it does not suit everyone to admit.

Pygmalion was Shaw's greatest commercial success, and it became the basis of the film and the long-running musical *My Fair Lady*. The original story is recounted by the Roman poet Ovid in his *Metamorphoses*. Pygmalion created a woman, Galatea, more perfect than the women around him. In Shaw's version, Higgins, a professor of phonetics – 'the science of speech' – conducts an experiment. He takes a flower-girl and turns her into a duchess. Higgins is an intriguing eccentric, but a confirmed old bachelor who shrinks from any emotional engagement. Eliza has our sympathy in her dependence on her teacher, and even more when she asserts her freedom from him. Shaw tells us that, despite attraction, Galatea 'never does quite like Pygmalion; his relationship to her is much too god-like to be agreeable'. The characters and the plot are a means to an end – the sheer amusement and delight of the dramatic experience, and the insights into ideas and behaviour which this affords. In *Pygmalion* we laugh at the verbal fireworks between Higgins and Eliza; what becomes of the characters is of secondary importance.

Shaw attacks a variety of normal assumptions of his predominantly middle-class audience. While his aim as a dramatist is to entertain us, Shaw also wanted to instruct us, to make us share his concern for the poor and underprivileged, and his wish for social change. His means is a light-hearted satire; as we laugh we are forced to re-examine our ideas, and perhaps to question whether they are based on reality and reason, or merely on custom and prejudice.

This play was first published in 1913. Bear in mind the great changes in society which have taken place since then. How did people manage without the welfare state? The family, and the charity of the wealthier classes, were important factors in the lives of the poor. How have our ideas and ideals changed? Before the First World War (1914–1918) most people were Christian. What effect would this have had on their behaviour? For example, marriage and family ties were regarded as sacred and binding, parents had 'rights'; it was good to be charitable, but wrong to give money to someone who would put it to a bad use, or to support someone in an immoral lifestyle. Whilst not everyone practised this moral code, they at least paid lip-service to it, and certainly considered it normal and right. If you remember that you are looking at a rather different culture than the present one, you should not find it too difficult to see what Shaw is mocking.

Doolittle – appropriately named – asks for his 'rights as a father'; we can see that he is to entertain us at length, for Pickering gives him the centre of the stage, saying 'The floor is yours'. We soon see that he is a spokesman for what we might call an alternative morality; he uses the terms of the usual one, but with a different, often a contrary meaning. Here he does not intend, as we suppose, to reclaim his daughter, but to sell her! Surely this is shocking, not comic? The reversal of what we expect takes us by surprise and this makes us laugh. The point is developed as, far from being worried about the men's motives, he reveals that dishonourable intentions would simply put the price up. Doolittle's arguments are a strictly logical development of an absurd or unacceptable premise, and have the effect of piling absurdity on absurdity, making us laugh more. What else do they do? Look at the response of Higgins and Pickering, whose dramatic function is to put to Doolittle the points which immediately spring to our minds. They are drawn into debate with him, and we see, first, their sympathies gained to a certain extent, as Higgins admits to feeling 'a sort of rough justice in his claim', then enthusiasm – 'this is irresistible', and lastly the acknowledgement that 'if we listen to this man another minute, we shall have no convictions left'. Although this is obviously humorous, we are meant to seriously reconsider our assumptions, and to ask ourselves whether our attitudes might not be different if we were in Doolittle's place, and whether we, too, might say of some points of morality, 'can't afford them'.

Doolittle battles on in the hope of payment, and advances the argument that he should be given money because he is 'undeserving'. Why is this funny? What are the grounds he gives for his claim? Absurd though his reason is – that it's harder for him to obtain charity because of people's moral scruples, and the development of it – that he doesn't eat less than a 'deserving man' and 'I drink a lot more' – we are attracted by the warmth of Shaw's acknowledgement of common human needs shared by the rogues and the righteous alike, not only for food but for the things extra to bare subsistence, represented here by 'cheerfulness and a song and a band when I feel low'.

Doolittle's rhetoric is having its effect on his – and Shaw's – audience. Offered not a mere five pounds, but a position of importance (and what are we to suppose Shaw's opinion of the holders of these positions to be, if Doolittle is seen as a suitable candidate for them?), what is his reply? Do you think most of the audience would make a similar reply? Would they be likely to immediately understand it? What are Shaw's feelings about Doolittle's attitude? We feel his sympathy for Doolittle's obvious enjoyment of his way of life, his 'station in society', the 'only one that has any ginger in it' for him. We see that those outside the middle-class pale of respectability may still have qualities of their own to recommend them.

The five pounds is conceded, and Pickering voices our fears about the use to which Doolittle will put it. What are we thinking of by 'bad use'? What does the term suggest to Doolittle? Why is this funny? 'Saving' would normally be considered a good thing for a poor man to do, because it is prudent behaviour; Doolittle points out that this could lead to idleness, which is understood to be bad, but by spending it he ensures that he will have to work again 'same as if I'd never had it'. This crazy garbling of well-worn phrases – 'live idle', 'pauperize', 'giving pleasure to ourselves and employment to others' – used in arguments about giving or withholding charitable help to the poor, is bound to make us reconsider our own views; are they really as sensible and unprejudiced as we think? Doolittle's refusal of the ten pounds is unlikely, but it allows Shaw to conclude the celebration of the sort of 'happiness' Doolitle represents – that of the moment fully enjoyed.

There remains a scruple in Pickering's mind about 'encouraging immorality'. Who does he imply would benefit most from the marriage by his question 'Why don't you marry that missus of yours?' What does Doolittle reply? How does Shaw intend us to react to this? Although there were benefits to be gained from marriage, it is sadly true that at that time marriage certainly gave a man 'a hold' on a woman, and he had no longer any need at all 'to be agreeable to her'. Whatever our moral views, when confronted by Doolittle, we must acknowledge the practical wisdom of his lady, and reflect on the unequal rights of men and women in marriage at that time. The serious note lightens in the exuberant burst of his advice to Higgins, but a trace of bitterness enters the humour as he ends triumphantly with what we feel must be the quotation of popular sentiments of the time 'but better her than you, because you're a man, and she's only a woman and don't know how to be happy anyhow'.

Assignment

Read the following extract from Brecht's *The Caucasian Chalk Circle*. What exactly is Azdak's role at this point? How does Grusha come to assume the centre stage and with what effect?

THE LAWYERS [*approaching Azdak, who stands up expectantly*]: An absolutely ridiculous case, Your Worship. The accused has abducted the child and refuses to hand it over.

AZDAK [*stretching out his hand, and glancing at Grusha*]: A most attractive person. [*He receives more money.*] I open the proceedings and demand the absolute truth. [*To Grusha*] Especially from you.

THE FIRST LAWYER: High Court of Justice! Blood, as the saying goes, is thicker than water. This old proverb . . .

AZDAK: The Court wants to know the lawyer's fee.

THE FIRST LAWYER *[surprised]*: I beg your pardon? *[Azdak rubs his thumb and index finger.]* Oh, I see. 500 piastres, Your Worship, is the answer to the Court's somewhat unusual question.

AZDAK: Did you hear? The question is unusual. I ask it because I listen to you in a quite different way if I know you are good.

THE FIRST LAWYER *[bowing]*: Thank you, Your Worship. High Court of Justice! Of all bonds the bonds of blood are the strongest. Mother and child – is there a more intimate relationship? Can one tear a child from its mother? High Court of Justice! She has conceived it in the holy ecstasies of love. She has carried it in her womb. She has fed it with her blood. She has borne it with pain. High Court of Justice! It has been observed, Your Worship, how even the wild tigress, robbed of her young, roams restless through the mountains, reduced to a shadow. Nature herself . . .

AZDAK *[interrupting, to Grusha]*: What's your answer to all this and anything else the lawyer might have to say?

GRUSHA: He's mine.

AZDAK: Is that all? I hope you can prove it. In any case, I advise you to tell me why you think the child should be given to you.

GRUSHA: I've brought him up 'according to my best knowledge and conscience'. I always found him something to eat. Most of the time he had a roof over his head. And I went to all sorts of trouble for him. I had expenses, too. I didn't think of my own comfort. I brought up the child to be friendly with everyone. And from the beginning I taught him to work as well as he could. But he's still very small.

THE FIRST LAWYER: Your Worship, it is significant that the person herself doesn't claim any bond of blood between herself and this child.

AZDAK: The Court takes note.

THE FIRST LAWYER: Thank you, Your Worship. Please permit a woman who has suffered much – who has already lost her husband and now also has to fear the loss of her child – to address a few words to you. Her Highness, Natella Abashvili . . .

THE GOVERNOR'S WIFE *[quietly]*: A most cruel fate, sir, forces me to ask you to return my beloved child. It's not for me to describe to you the tortures of a bereaved mother's soul, the anxiety, the sleepless nights, the . . .

THE SECOND LAWYER *[exploding]*: It's outrageous the way this woman is treated. She's not allowed to enter her husband's palace. The revenue of her estates is blocked. She is told cold-bloodedly that it's tied to the heir. She can't do anything without the child. She can't even pay her lawyers. *[To the first lawyer who, desperate about this outburst, makes frantic gestures to stop him speaking]*: Dear Illo Shuboladze, why shouldn't it be divulged now that it's the Abashvili estates that are at stake?

THE FIRST LAWYER: Please, Honoured Sandro Obolodze! We had agreed . . . *[To Azdak]*: Of course it is correct that the trial will also decide whether our noble client will obtain the right to dispose of the large Abashvili estates. I say 'also' on purpose, because in the foreground stands the human tragedy of a mother, as Natella Abashvili has rightly explained at the beginning of her moving statement. Even if Michael Abashvili were *not* the heir to the estates, he would still be the dearly beloved child of my client.

AZDAK: Stop! The Court is touched by the mention of the estates. It's a proof of human feeling.

THE SECOND LAWYER: Thanks, Your Worship. Dear Illo Shuboladze, in any case we can prove that the person who took possession of the child is not the child's mother. Permit me to lay before the Court the bare facts. By an unfortunate chain of circumstances, the child, Michael Abashvili, was left behind while his mother was making her escape. Grusha, the palace kitchenmaid, was present on this Easter Sunday and was observed busying herself with the child . . .

THE COOK: All her mistress was thinking about was what kind of dresses she would take along.

THE SECOND LAWYER *[unmoved]*: Almost a year later Grusha turned up in a mountain village with a child, and there entered into matrimony with . . .

AZDAK: How did you get into that mountain village?

GRUSHA: On foot, Your Worship. And he was mine.

SIMON: I am the father, Your Worship.

THE COOK: I had him in my care for five piastres, Your Worship.

THE SECOND LAWYER: This man is engaged to Grusha, High Court of Justice, and for this reason his testimony is not reliable.

AZDAK: Are you the man she married in the mountain village?

SIMON: No, Your Worship, she married a peasant.

AZDAK *[winking at Grusha]*: Why? *[Pointing at Simon]*: Isn't he any good in bed? Tell the truth.

GRUSHA: We didn't get that far. I married because of the child, so that he should have a roof over his head. *[Pointing at Simon]* He was in the war, Your Worship.

AZDAK: And now he wants you again, eh?

SIMON: I want to state in evidence . . .

GRUSHA *[angrily]*: I am no longer free, Your Worship.

AZDAK: And the child, you claim, is the result of whoring? *[Grusha does not answer.]* I'm going to ask you a question: What kind of child is it? Is it one of those ragged street-urchins? Or is it a child from a well-to-do family?

GRUSHA *[angrily]*: It's an ordinary child.

AZDAK: I mean, did he have fine features from the beginning?

GRUSHA: He had a nose in his face.

AZDAK: He had a nose in his face. I consider that answer of yours to be important. They say of me that once, before passing judgement, I went out and sniffed at a rosebush. Tricks of this kind are necessary nowadays. I'll cut things short now, and listen no longer to your lies. *[To Grusha]*: Especially yours. *[To the group of defendants]*: I can imagine what you've cooked up between you to cheat me. You're swindlers.

GRUSHA *[suddenly]*: I can quite understand your wanting to cut it short, having seen what you received!

AZDAK: Shut up! Did I receive anything from you?

GRUSHA *[while the cook tries to restrain her]*: Because I haven't got anything.

AZDAK: Quite true. I never get a thing from starvelings. I might just as well starve myself. You want justice, but do you want to pay for it? When you go to a butcher you know you have to pay. But to the Judge you go as though to a funeral supper.

SIMON *[loudly]*: 'When the horse was shod, the horsefly stretched out its leg', as the saying is.

AZDAK *[eagerly accepting the challenge]*: 'Better a treasure in the sewer than a stone in the mountain stream.'

SIMON: '"A fine day. Let's go fishing," said the angler to the worm.'

AZDAK: '"I'm my own master," said the servant, and cut off his foot.'

SIMON: '"I love you like a father," said the Czar to the peasant, and had the Czarevitch's head chopped off.'

AZDAK: 'A fool's worst enemy is himself.'

SIMON: But 'a fart has no nose'.

AZDAK: Fined ten piastres for indecent language in Court. That'll teach you what Justice is.

GRUSHA: That's a fine kind of Justice. You jump on us because we don't talk so refined as that lot with their lawyers.

AZDAK: Exactly. The likes of you are too stupid. It's only right that you should get it in the neck.

GRUSHA: Because you want to pass the child on to her. She who is too refined even to know how to change its nappies! You don't know any more about Justice than I do, that's clear.

AZDAK: There's something in that. I'm an ignorant man. I haven't even a decent pair of trousers under my robe. See for yourself. With me, everything goes on food and drink. I was educated in a convent school. Come to think of it, I'll fine you ten piastres, too. For contempt of Court. What's more, you're a very silly girl to turn me against you, instead of making eyes at me and wagging your backside a bit to keep me in a good temper. Twenty piastres!

GRUSHA: Even if it were thirty, I'd tell you what I think of your justice, you drunken onion! How dare you talk to me as though you were the cracked Isaiah on a church window! When they pulled you out of your mother it wasn't planned that you'd rap her over the knuckles for pinching a little bowl of corn from somewhere! Aren't you ashamed of yourself when you see how afraid I am of you? But you've let yourself become their servant. So that their houses are not taken away, because they've stolen them. Since when do houses belong to bed-bugs? But you're on the look-out, otherwise they couldn't drag our men into their wars. You bribe-taker!
[Azdak gets up. He begins to beam. With a little hammer he knocks on the table half-heartedly as if to get silence. But as Grusha's scolding continues, he only beats time with it.]
I've no respect for you. No more than for a thief or a murderer with a knife, who does what he wants. You can take the child away from me, a hundred against one, but I tell you one thing: for a profession like yours, they ought to choose only bloodsuckers and men who hate children. As a punishment. To make them sit in judgement over their fellow men, which is worse than swinging from the gallows.

Notes

Imagine the scene as if it were dramatized. Hear the voices of the lawyers whining the rhetoric that Natella's conduct has denied: 'of all the bonds the bonds of blood are the strongest. Mother and child – is there a more intimate relationship?' The lawyers' greed is too urgent to remain disguised: 'The revenue of her estates is blocked. She is told cold-bloodedly that it's tied to the heir', and Natella's grief is absurdly over-rehearsed. So, by what they say and the way that they say it, the party technically in the right is distanced from sympathy.

Azdak has just escaped hanging, and resumes the role of anarchic champion of justice with his customary, ironic self-deprecation: 'The court takes note'. His sardonic interruptions appear indiscriminate, and this acts to increase tension by further testing Grusha's resolve.

Grusha is never over-awed by the case, power or presence ranged against her. She gradually becomes angry as what she perceives as natural justice is threatened by selfish interest. Her final speech in this extract has the moral authority which the audience believes – but is not sure – will win the case: the responsibility of judgement, she says, is so awesome that no ordinary, fallible mortal can possibly be worthy of it. The climax of her accusation has a profound dramatic effect. What now will Azdak do?

'Open-ended' questions

There follow some examples of assignments that illustrate a more open-ended approach to a piece of writing. The play is regarded as a catalyst – a starting-point, or stimulus – to which the reader brings life and meaning. Here, the emphasis is on originality and vitality of response, and there is greater freedom to develop ideas. With coursework intended specifically for the English Literature file, it should be remembered that responses ought to be firmly rooted in the text – that is, your reader must be able to see clearly the connection between the play and writing you do. It must be made clear that the content and quality of your writing have depended upon an initial reading. To indicate the freedom and the potential of this approach, here are some general suggestions for writing, which can be adapted to provide models for assignments on particular plays with which you are familiar:

– imaginary interviews with characters (scripted, or improvised and recorded),
– diaries kept by characters,
– alternative endings,
– a scene inserted, involving minor or major characters,
– comparisons between performances, or between stage and screen versions,
– transcript of group discussion, with added commentary,
– personal free writing inspired by the drama,
– suggestions for production.

Here is an extract from the play *Billy Liar* by Keith Waterhouse and Willis Hall. Billy is exactly that, and at this point in the play it suits him to admit it – almost. The coursework assignment set is an example of an exercise designed to reveal the student's imaginative understanding of the drama and to encourage a creative response.

BILLY: Sit down, darling. *[Barbara sits on the couch.]* Darling, are you still coming to tea this afternoon?

BARBARA: Of course.

BILLY: Because there are some things I want to tell you.

BARBARA: What things, Billy?

BILLY: You know what you said the other night – about loving me? Even if I were a criminal.

BARBARA: Well?

BILLY: You said you'd love me even if I'd murdered your mother.

BARBARA *[suspiciously]*: Well?

BILLY: I wonder if you'll still love me when you hear what I've got to say. You see – well, you know that I've got a fairly vivid imagination, don't you?

BARBARA: Well, you have to have if you're going to be a script-writer, don't you?

BILLY: Well, being a script-writer, I'm perhaps – at times – a bit inclined to let my imagination run away with me. As you know. *[Barbara is even more aloof than usual.]* You see, the thing is, if we're going to have our life together – and that cottage – and little Billy and little Barbara and the lily pond and all that . . . Well, there's some things we've got to get cleared up.

BARBARA: What things?

BILLY: Some of the things I've been telling you.

BARBARA: Do you mean that you've been telling me lies?

BILLY: Well, not lies exactly . . . But I suppose I've been, well, exaggerating some things. Being a script-writer . . . For instance, there's that business about my father. Him being a sea-captain. On a petrol tanker.

BARBARA: You mean he's not on a petrol tanker?

BILLY: He's not even in the navy.

BARBARA: Well, what is he?

BILLY: He's in the removal business.

BARBARA: And what about him being a prisoner-of-war? And that tunnel? And the medal? Don't say that was all lies?

BILLY: Yes. *[Barbara turns away abruptly.]* Are you cross?

BARBARA: No – not cross. Just disappointed. It sounds as though you were ashamed of your father.

BILLY: I'm not ashamed. I'm not – I'm not!

BARBARA: Otherwise why say he was a prisoner-of-war? What was he?

BILLY: A conscientious obj . . . *[He checks himself.]* He wasn't anything. He wasn't fit. He has trouble with his knee.

BARBARA: The knee he's supposed to have been shot in I suppose.

BILLY: Yes. Another thing, we haven't got a budgie, or cat. And I didn't make the furniture . . . Not all of it, anyway.

BARBARA: How many other lies have you been telling me?

BILLY: My sister.

BARBARA: Don't tell me you haven't got a sister.

BARBARA: I did have. But she's dead. If you're still coming this afternoon they never talk about her.
[Barbara remains silent, her head still turned away.]
You remind me of her . . . If you're not coming, I'll understand . . . I'm just not good enough for you, Barbara . . . if you want to give me the engagement ring back – I'll understand.

BARBARA *[turning towards him]*: Don't be cross with yourself, Billy, I forgive you.

Assignment

How well does the scene illustrate the basic idea of the play – that Billy is a compulsive liar? What do you think Billy is trying to arrange in this scene? How do Barbara's reactions help or hinder him? Continue the dialogue so as to bring out how you think Billy might respond to Barbara's forgiveness.

Notes

Write one paragraph in answer to each of the questions in the assignment. Show how extravagantly Billy has lied, repeatedly, about his father; and how, even when admitting his invention, he tries to explain it away – and finds himself lying automatically. He tries to excuse himself by referring to the script-writer's imagination that sometimes gets the better of him. On the defensive, having admitted to so much, Billy finds himself embroidering the boring truth with the emotionally dramatic idea that his father was a 'conscientious obj . . .'. Billy is trying to get the ring back; he wants Barbara to break off the engagement. Read the extract again, concentrating on Billy's attempts to manoeuvre Barbara into deserting him because he is unworthy of her love. How would Billy feel when Barbara says 'Don't be cross with yourself, Billy, I forgive you'? Continue the conversation, remembering to keep the characters and circumstances as they are given to you in the extract. Your extension of the scene should flow naturally from what has gone before. It is a good idea to write several versions, until you are sure you have the style and content right. Do not look at the play itself at this point, simply try to write dialogue for these characters. What might Billy say next? Anything, just so long as he gets the ring back? And why might he be so keen to get it back just at the moment? For example.

BILLY: Er, well, that's good of you, Barbara. I don't deserve it.

BARBARA: I know, Billy.

BILLY: I'm sorry I've exaggerated everything. It's very embarrassing. Makes me feel a bit small somehow.

BARBARA: Good. But we can kiss and make up now, Billy, can't we?

BILLY: Yes, darling. *[Goes to sit beside her. Takes her hands in his.]* And you don't mind about the ring?

BARBARA: What do you mean, Billy?

BILLY: I knew you'd see it like that. After all, it's the thought that's behind it that counts, isn't it? The ring itself is just a token. We can get a real one later.

Assignment

Read the final scene of *The Caucasian Chalk Circle* by Bertolt Brecht. Write two accounts of the proceedings in Azdak's court, one of which is sympathetic to the judgement and the judge, and the other of which recognizes the claim of the real mother and accepts the arguments of her lawyers.

Notes

Each account should make full use of the text. Use the information given in the scene, and only add embellishments if you are convinced that they are consistent with the scene itself, that is, if they clarify or emphasize what you believe the playwright intended.

There is plenty of material. The first account might stress the disparity between the condition of the servant girl and the Governor's wife, tell Grusha's story as the court heard it, and go on to relate the past behaviour of the real mother, the speeches of her lawyers, and her willingness to tear the child apart. The account is not intended to be dispassionate, and so the tone and style will partly convey the appropriate judgement. Imagine yourself, for example, to be the Cook, one of Grusha's fellow servants, writing to her family in the country about the events in the city. What would she make of the conduct of Natella and her lawyers? Perhaps a healthy mistrust of Azdak's eccentricity might be mingled with a grudging respect for his courage and wisdom? How would the Cook react to the curious antics of the judge in refusing to divorce the old couple who have disliked each other from the very beginning, but who divorced Grusha from the peasant she married in the mountain village to provide a roof and a name for the child? Alternatively, you could write the story as Simon might tell it to his comrades, or even as an elderly, still drunken and unpredictable Azdak might tell it years hence – to anyone who would listen.

In opposition to this, affronted by the indignity of an inebriate clerk masquerading as a judge and denying the God-given rights of blood and property, the second account would see the chalk circle as a charlatan's trick to deprive the rightful owners of what is truly theirs. The deliberate mistaking of identity and confiscation of estates adds to the miscarriage of justice. The lawyers themselves would give a suitably outraged version of this travesty of justice. One of the farmers whom Azdak fired on account of their lack of faith in the miracle-working St Banditus would provide a malicious and spiteful report of the judgement – for the learned gentleman who will doubtless eventually assume the judgement seat. Perhaps even a grizzled Ironshirt, mourning the death of plunder, in later years would recall the last public moments of the man who talked like a carpet-weaver and became a legend.

Think yourself into the role of observer so that you visualize the courtroom drama and refer to its detail as if you really had been present. Your writings will take on characteristics of the personalities and viewpoints you have assumed, and will be convincing because of this.

Assignment

What do you think it is important for a producer of *A Midsummer Night's Dream* to bear in mind when considering the last act of the play?

Notes

The question is not quite as open as it might seem. You are not asked simply to give your personal prescription for a production – which is difficult enough – but you are required to write about what it is important for a producer to understand and interpret. An introductory section of your work should show your recognition of the synthetic nature of this scene, bringing together as it does the lovers reconciled in the ceremony and solemnity of the court of Theseus and Hippolyta, their follies mirrored by the 'very tragical mirth' of the mechanicals' performance of Pyramus and Thisbe, and the scene presided over by spirits offering blessing and heralding the dawn. Once you have demonstrated that you are clear about what this act of several scenes does with the various strands of the plot, and how it draws them together into one meaning, then you can allow your 'seething brain' to give to 'airy nothing/A local habitation and a name' and say how you see the production taking shape. You can of course recall any performance you may have seen, and better still say what you would attempt to do yourself. Practical considerations should enter at this point: under what constraints and conditions are you operating, in your discussion, of setting, costumes, backdrop, lighting, music and dance? And what are your assumptions about the character of the court, the lovers, the fairies and the mechanicals – as well as the particular interpretations your actors could bring to, for example, Bottom, Oberon, Puck, Theseus? What will bring your coursework alive will be your ability to communicate an awareness and enthusiasm for the dramatic possibilities of the script.

Assignment

Write a new ending to Shaw's *Pygmalion*.

Notes

Eliza, despite her surface performance, is mentally caught between the lower and the middle class, and is now truly acceptable to neither. Without marrying her to any of the characters already introduced, see if you can continue the story. Perhaps she will indeed teach phonetics and rival Higgins – or even embarrass him by publishing her story. Read Shaw's sequel to the play, and try to think of less romantic possibilities.

Assignment

Imagine that you are in the position of Eliza – someone offers to change you in such a way that you become acceptable to people who would normally be hesitant or reluctant to accept you. What would you wish to happen, and how would you expect circumstances to develop?

Notes

Invent a character who plays a similar role to that of Higgins – someone who wants to conduct some kind of social experiment, and who enjoys the excitement of the game and the power he acquires. Using a contemporary setting, write one or two short scenes for your play, showing some of the difficulties you encounter. Indicate clearly the results of your experiment.

Assignment

Imagine that you are Eliza Doolittle before Professor Higgins has taken charge of you. Bearing in mind the information given in the play about your family and your lodgings, write an account of the life you lead and how you see yourself and your future.

Notes

Your task is to project yourself imaginatively into the character and circumstances given, and what you write should be consistent with this. Look at the way Eliza speaks and what this tells you about how she thinks. Refer closely to evidence in the play which provides you with some of your material.

General coursework assignments

The following exercises can be adapted to suit virtually any play you are studying. The assignments are designed to provide written work. Some of them require group preparation, and, if it is possible to include a record of the practical element, then this might also be accepted for assessment. Tapes and video-recordings could be used to support and illustrate what you have written.

1 Imagine you are the principal character of a play. Before an audience, real or imaginary, explain your feelings and justify your conduct. Record what you find yourself saying, and make a transcript – or re-write the speech that evolves from the improvisation, commenting on the process as you find the speech taking shape.

2 With some friends, take turns to role-play minor characters who are being interviewed about events that have taken place. Try to develop a sense of a world that is wider than that of the scripted scenes, and yet introduce nothing that is not consistent with the play proper. Tape and script the final version, including in your coursework evidence of the exercise in its various stages, with comment and explanation where appropriate.

3 Rehearse a scene from a play. Note the problems that occurred and how you dealt with them. What exactly did the rehearsal teach you about the play? This exercise can provide a detailed, thorough piece of work that will reveal the depth of your knowledge of the play as well as your appreciation of it.

4 Write extracts from the diaries of several characters so as to bring out their differing reactions to the same event.

5 Write a scene that you would like to insert in the play. Explain why you would like to include it, and what you think it might contribute.

6 Take a scene that is significant, but is not the climax of the play. Extend the scene slightly, introducing no further complications to the plot. Concentrate on the characters' language.

7 Use a scene from a play as the stimulus for some imaginative writing of your own. This could be in the form of drama, but it does not have to be – providing the connection is clear.

8 See if you can construct some visual/schematic/diagrammatic means of representing the movement of the play, its structure, or the relationships that exist between the characters. What do you find this way of looking at the drama highlights?

9 Write out a passage of the play and experiment with the dialogue, commenting on the effect of any changes you have tried. What, if anything, have you found out about the original in the process?

10 Discuss, in detail, with references and quotations, one of the following aspects of the play: characters, and characterization (the way our sense of the individuals is built up by what they say and the way that they say it, by what they do and by the way they react); the structure of the plot (the way the story unfolds); the setting of the play in time and place; themes (recurring ideas and concerns); atmosphere and tone; dialogue.

Coursework assignments on particular plays

The following assignments in drama are suitable for inclusion in a coursework file in English or English literature. The notes are provided so as to help you to appreciate the possibilities of the various forms of assignment. The discussion is limited to particular plays so as to encourage you to read in support of the use of these notes, and to illustrate the demands and the potential of the different approaches to the same text.

1 The plots of television soap operas have been affected by a government policy drive to combat the spread of AIDS. You are one of the writing team for any popular series. Taking up the story from where it is at the moment, introduce the changes you think might be required.

Notes

Your instructions, as a script-writer, are to make the threat real and not hypothetical or distant. Sympathetic characters will now have attitudes that reinforce the required pattern of sexual relationships. Behaviour which does not conform to the new guidelines on monogamy and fidelity is undesirable and dangerous, and characters who cannot be adapted to the alterations may have to be written out of the series.

2 Write your own school series for television performance.

Notes

Schools are rarely portrayed realistically on television. Try to introduce elements that you feel have been lacking in recent drama. Remember that you are using experience to create something that is heightened and transformed, and do not be too dependent either on the detail of your own setting or on the characters and preoccupations of your televisual models. This does not have to be the first episode. Briefly tell us where we are in the story, and then script the next instalment.

3 Read the following extract from I, 3 of *Antony and Cleopatra*. Write about opposing views of the way to keep the affection of the opposite sex.

CLEOPATRA: Where is he?

CHARMIAN *[an attendant]*: I did not see him since.

CLEOPATRA *[to another attendant]*:
See where he is, who's with him, what he does:
I did not send you. If you find him sad,
Say I am dancing; if in mirth, report
That I am sudden sick. Quick, and return.

CHARMIAN: Madam, methinks if you did love him dearly,
You do not hold the method, to enforce
The like from him.

CLEOPATRA: What should I do, I do not?

CHARMIAN: In each thing give him way, cross him in nothing.

CLEOPATRA: Thou teachest like a fool: the way to lose him.

Notes

Cleopatra, Queen of Egypt, is preparing to meet the man she loves, Mark Antony, the Roman general. Her charm has bewitched the old warrior, and he feels his character and independence sapped by this involvement with the beautiful queen. In this extract from Shakespeare's *Antony and Cleopatra*, Cleopatra demands that her servant find out Antony's mood, and report to him that she is in a contrasting mood. Cleopatra's theory of love seems to be that it is an attraction of opposites, and that a lover will lose interest if the object of desire and affection is dependable or passive. Her words imply that strife and uncertainty will keep love alive. This view is diametrically opposed to the advice of Charmian, her servant, who thinks that the mistress should please the master and so continue to command his affections.

The passage may be used as a starting-point for a general discussion on the subject of attraction and the tensions of relationship, or for accounts of behaviour you have observed, or provide a model for a sketch presenting a modern version of this kind of exchange.

4 'What a piece of work is man, how noble in reason, how

infinite in faculty, in form and moving how express and admirable, in action how like an angel, in apprehension how like a god: the beauty of the world, the paragon of animals. And yet, to me, what is this quintessence of dust? man delights not me'
Hamlet (II, 2).

In this quotation from Shakespeare's *Hamlet* the young Prince Hamlet utters his weariness of treacherous, rotten humanity. Take the impetus of the speech and consider it in a modern setting: an international conference of women meets to discuss the problems of the modern world, which appears either to be suffering or to be on the brink of various catastrophes: the destruction of the environment; disease and malnutrition; political oppression in various guises; international terrorism; religious fanaticism; global warfare threatening extinction. The delegates decide that all the outstanding problems of the time have one basic cause – human aggression, which they see as a male characteristic. As we have reached a stage in development where men are virtually unnecessary for the reproduction of the species and, moreover, threaten its survival, the conference votes that men should be considered biologically obsolete. Write a report from the conference, or a transcript of the debate.

The following plays are common to most of the GCSE syllabuses and reading lists. With each one are some suggested assignments. If none of these plays is in your own list, adapt a suitable assignment to a play you are studying and undertake it with the title of your own play in mind.

1 *Death of a Salesman* Arthur Miller

Write about the play's treatment of ambition and love.
In what ways is Willie's tragedy brought about by the standards of contemporary society?
Write a passage in which there is clash between a person's career and his domestic responsibilities. Base your answer on material in the play, and write it as a dramatic sketch (i.e. in dialogue) if you wish.
Examine any aspect of the play and say what it has told you of American life at the time.
What, for you, is the most moving scene in the play and why? Use quotations and summary to support your view.

2 *Macbeth* Shakespeare

Study the effect of Duncan's murder on Macbeth and Lady Macbeth. Examine how their relationship changes as the play progresses.

Show how Shakespeare creates an atmosphere of fear in any two scenes in the play.

Write a character study of any character apart from Macbeth and Lady Macbeth.

Summarize the effects and use of the supernatural in the play. What does it contribute to the dramatic effect of the play?

Drawing your ideas from events and situations in the play, write a passage about ambition and its effects, *or* on a relationship which leads to disaster, *or* on the practice of deception to achieve one's ends.

3 *An Inspector Calls* J. B. Priestley

Setting this play in today's world, using modern social conditions, attitudes and perhaps injustice, write a scene in which the connection between any of the main characters and the dead girl is revealed.

Write a clear summary of the most important scene in the play in your opinion.

Who do you find the most interesting character and why?

4 *Under Milk Wood* Dylan Thomas

This was first written as a play for radio. Bearing that in mind, do you think that the script presents any difficulties for a producer and his cast?

By reference to three or four sequences, bring out the qualities of humour inherent in the play. Which for you is the most entertaining of these sequences and why? You should refer closely to the extracts in question in your answer.

Write an imaginative passage, either in prose or dialogue, about gossip in your own area and its effects. You should derive your ideas from the play.

5 *Arms and the Man* George Bernard Shaw

Do you find this a romantic drama, or is Shaw encouraging laughter at the attitudes it portrays?

Write an appreciation of any one scene in the play which is either dramatic or pathetic or both.

This play – as with the *My Fair Lady* adaptation of *Pygmalion* –

was made into a musical. Indicate the qualities in *Arms and the Man* which, in your opinion, would make it a good musical comedy.

Re-write the ending of the play giving it a different but convincing twist.

6 *Hobson's Choice* Harold Brighouse

Whom do you sympathize with in the play, at what point exactly, and why?

Write an account of the most dramatic scene in the play, bringing out its effective qualities.

Imagine that you are a character in the play. Tell the story of the action as you see it.

7 *The Importance of Being Earnest* Oscar Wilde

What aspects of society do you think Wilde is making fun of?

Write an appreciation of Wilde's use of contrast in the presentation of his characters.

Which do you consider the funniest scene in the play and why?

Basing your ideas on the obsession of Gwendolen and Cecily, write a passage – either in prose or dialogue – to show that a fixed idea can make someone behave in a silly or even a dangerous manner.

8 *The Merchant of Venice* Shakespeare

Which merchant of Venice interests you most and why?

Which character or characters in the play do you sympathize with and why?

Write an appreciation of either the courtroom scene *or* a romantic scene *or* a humorous scene.

Imagine you are present in court when Shylock demands his bond. Write an account of the proceedings for your local paper, using headlines if you wish, but basing your story entirely on what happens in court.

9 *The Caucasian Chalk Circle* Bertolt Brecht

What is the point of the first scene in the play? If you were a producer, would you leave it in or cut it?

10 *Murder in the Cathedral* T. S. Eliot

What are your reactions to the arguments of the Knights at the end of the play? Why do you think the language is made different from the verse in the rest of the play?

Write an account of your reactions to the character and attitudes of Becket, saying why you feel as you do.

In what ways does the chorus contribute to the dramatic action of the play?

Write a passage in which the individual triumphs against odds or in which he/she suffers defeat at the hands of those in power. Your answer must be based on ideas or situations in the play.

11 *Journey's End* R. C. Sherriff

Do you think the play is too dated to mean much to people nowadays?

Indicate clearly in what ways this play condemns war or the situation in which soldiers find themselves.

Which of the soldiers seems to you to be the most convincing and why?

The play ends in mid-battle. Write an alternative ending, based on the dramatic action and without losing the realism of it.

12 *The Rivals* R. B. Sheridan

In what ways do you find this an enjoyable and exuberant play?

Give an account of the plot of the play, bringing out clearly the humour involved.

Write a speech of about twenty lines for Mrs Malaprop in which you bring out her misuse of language. You should find some new 'malapropisms' of your own to include in it.

Write about any aspect of the play which interests you and which is not covered by the questions above.

13 *Twelfth Night* Shakespeare

Write about a scene you found sad as well as funny, and explain your reactions as fully as you can.

Compare and contrast Viola and Olivia *and* Sir Toby and Sir Andrew. How far is the drama (and the humour) of the play dependent on the idea of mistaken identity?

Write a report for Olivia on the tormenting of Malvolio, basing it entirely on what happens in the play, and saying whether you agree or disagree (with reasons) with the treatment he suffers.

Write a passage, based on situations within the play, which shows that narrow-mindedness gets what it deserves.

14 *Romeo and Juliet* Shakespeare

What events in the play combine to make it a tragedy? Refer closely to particular scenes in your answer.

Who is the most attractive character in the play and why?
Basing your ideas on the action of the play, write an alternative ending in which either Romeo or Juliet or both survive.
The scene in which Mercutio is killed should be read carefully. Using material in that scene, give it a modern setting in a big city and write it dramatically in the language of today.

15 *The Real Inspector Hound* Tom Stoppard

Read this with a group of friends before you answer. When you have done so, write a passage saying what it is about the play that appeals to you.
Consider individual lines and characters in the play that made you laugh. What do you think you are being made to laugh at?
In what ways does this play differ from a thriller. Indicate its nature by referring to the text.
Imagine that you are one of the characters in the play. Write an account of the action from your own viewpoint.

16 *The Winslow Boy* Terence Rattigan

Show how, as the play progresses, the focus of attention shifts from the boy himself and his alleged crime. What do you think is the point of this?
Who do you find the most sympathetic character in the play and why?
Write an account of the most dramatic scene in the play.
Imagine that you are a television reporter. Update the action of the play to the present time, and write down (in dialogue) an interview you have had with the boy's father.

Coursework assignments with stimulus passage

Here are open questions to encourage some free writing which also has an obvious connection with the stimulus passage.

Assignment

Read the extract from Act I of Oscar Wilde's *The Importance of Being Earnest* and comment on the comedy of the interview of this eligible young man by the over-powering Lady Bracknell. Tell the story of the conversation in your own words, pointing out what you have found out about what impresses the prospective mother-in-law, and what convinces her that the match is an unsuitable one. Write an alternative, modern version of such an interview.

LADY BRACKNELL *[sitting down]*: You can take a seat, Mr Worthing. *[Looks in her pocket for note book and pencil.]*

JACK: Thank you, Lady Bracknell, I prefer standing.

LADY BRACKNELL *[pencil and note book in hand]*: I feel bound to tell you that you are not down on my list of eligible young men, although I have the same list as the dear Duchess of Bolton has. We work together in fact. However, I am quite ready to enter your name, should your answers be what a really affectionate mother requires. Do you smoke?

JACK: Well, yes, I must admit I smoke.

LADY BRACKNELL: I'm glad to hear it. A man should always have an occupation of some kind. There are too many idle men in London as it is. How old are you?

JACK: Twenty-nine.

LADY BRACKNELL: A very good age to be married at. I have always been of the opinion that a man who desires to get married should know either everything or nothing. Which do you know?

JACK *[after some hesitation]*: I know nothing, Lady Bracknell.

LADY BRACKNELL: I am pleased to hear it. I do not approve of anything that tampers with natural ignorance. Ignorance is like a delicate exotic fruit; touch it and the bloom is gone. The whole theory of modern education is radically unsound. Fortunately in England, at any rate, education produces no effect whatsoever. If it did, it would prove a serious danger to the upper classes, and probably lead to acts of violence in Grosvenor Square. What is your income?

JACK: Between seven and eight thousand a year.

LADY BRACKNELL *[makes a note in her book]*: In land or in investments?

JACK: In investments, chiefly.

LADY BRACKNELL: That is satisfactory. What between the duties expected of one during one's lifetime, and the duties exacted from one after one's death, land has ceased to be either a profit or a pleasure. It gives one position and prevents one from keeping it up. That's all that can be said about land.

JACK: I have a country house with some land, of course, attached to it, about fifteen hundred acres, I believe; but I don't depend on that for my real income. In fact, as far as I can make out, the poachers are the only people who make anything out of it.

LADY BRACKNELL: A country house! How many bedrooms? Well, that point can be cleared up afterwards. You have a town house, I hope. A girl with a simple, unspoiled nature, like Gwendolen, could hardly be expected to reside in the country.

JACK: Well, I own a house in Belgrave Square, but it is let by the year to Lady Bloxham. Of course, I can get it back whenever I like, at six months' notice.

LADY BRACKNELL: Lady Bloxham? I don't know her.

JACK: Oh, she goes about very little. She is a lady considerably advanced in years.

LADY BRACKNELL: Ah, nowadays that is no guarantee of respectability of character. What number in Belgrave Square?

JACK: 149

LADY BRACKNELL [shaking her head]: The unfashionable side. I thought there was something. However, that could easily be altered.

JACK: Do you mean the fashion, or the side.

LADY BRACKNELL [sternly]: Both, if necessary, I presume. What are your politics?

JACK: Well, I am afraid I really have none. I am a Liberal Unionist.

LADY BRACKNELL: Oh, they count as Tories. They dine with us. Or come in the evening, at any rate. Now to minor matters. Are your parents living?

JACK: I have lost both my parents.

LADY BRACKNELL: To lose one parent, Mr Worthing, may be regarded as a misfortune; to lose both looks like carelessness. Who was your father? He was evidently a man of some wealth. Was he born in what the Radical papers call the purple of commerce, or did he rise from the ranks of the aristocracy?

JACK: I am afraid I really don't know. The fact is, Lady Bracknell, I said I had lost my parents. It would be nearer the truth to say that my parents seem to have lost me . . . I don't actually know who I am by birth. I was . . . well, I was found.

LADY BRACKNELL: Found!

JACK: The late Mr Thomas Cardew, an old gentleman of a very charitable and kindly disposition, found me, and gave me the name of

Worthing, because he happened to have a first-class ticket for Worthing in his pocket at the time. Worthing is a place in Sussex. It is a seaside resort.

LADY BRACKNELL: Where did the charitable gentleman who had a first-class ticket for this seaside resort find you?

JACK [gravely]: In a hand-bag.

LADY BRACKNELL: A hand-bag?

JACK [very seriously]: Yes, Lady Bracknell. I was in a hand-bag – a somewhat large, black leather hand-bag, with handles to it – an ordinary hand-bag in fact.

LADY BRACKNELL: In what locality did this Mr James, or Thomas, Cardew come across this ordinary hand-bag?

JACK: In the cloak-room at Victoria station. It was given to him in mistake for his own.

LADY BRACKNELL: The cloak-room at Victoria station?

JACK: Yes. The Brighton line.

LADY BRACKNELL: The line is immaterial. Mr Worthing, I confess I feel somewhat bewildered by what you have just told me. To be born, or at any rate bred in a hand-bag, whether it had handles or not, seems to me to display a contempt for the ordinary decencies of family life that remind one of the worst excesses of the French Revolution. And I presume you know what that unfortunate movement led to? As for the particular locality in which the hand-bag was found, a cloak-room at a railway station might serve to conceal a social indiscretion – has probably, indeed, been used for that purpose before now – but it could hardly be regarded as an assured basis for a recognised position in good society.

JACK: May I ask you then what you would advise me to do? I need hardly say I would do anything in the world to ensure Gwendolen's happiness.

LADY BRACKNELL: I would strongly advise you, Mr Worthing, to try and acquire some relations as soon as possible, and to make a definite effort to produce at least one parent, of either sex, before the season is quite over.

JACK: Well, I don't see how I could possibly manage to do that. I can produce the hand-bag at any moment. It is in my dressing-room at home. I really think that should satisfy you, Lady Bracknell.

LADY BRACKNELL: Me, Sir! What has it to do with me? You can hardly imagine that I and Lord Bracknell would dream of allowing our only daughter – a girl brought up with utmost care – to marry into a cloak-room, and form an alliance with a parcel? Good morning, Mr Worthing! *[Lady Bracknell sweeps out in majestic indignation.]*

Assignment

Read Mark Antony's speech to the crowd after the murder of Julius Caesar (*Julius Caesar* III, 3). With a group of friends, read and rehearse the following scene. What potential has it for the creation of a sense of menace and mayhem? Imagine you are part of this mob; write your version of what happens. Pay particular attention to the atmosphere created by Shakespeare, and focus on the influence of each speaker and the way each is influenced by the prevailing mood.

When it is all over and the scene has ended, imagine that you are Mark Antony. Make an entry in your diary describing the assassination of Caesar, your reactions, your speech to the crowd, their reactions, and your hopes for the future.

CINNA: I dreamt to-night that I did feast with Caesar,
And things unluckily charge my fantasy.
I have no will to wander forth of doors,
Yet something leads me forth. *[Enter Plebeians.]*

FIRST PLEBEIAN: What is your name?

SECOND PLEBEIAN: Whither are you going?

THIRD PLEBEIAN: Where do you dwell?

FOURTH PLEBEIAN: Are you a married man or a bachelor?

SECOND PLEBEIAN: Answer every man directly.

FIRST PLEBEIAN: Ay, and briefly.

FOURTH PLEBEIAN: Ay, and wisely.

THIRD PLEBEIAN: Ay, and truly, you were best.

CINNA: What is my name? Whither am I going? Where do I dwell? Am I a married man or a bachelor? Then, to answer every man directly and briefly, wisely and truly: wisely, I say, I am a bachelor.

SECOND PLEBEIAN: That's as much as to say they are fools that marry. You'll bear me a bang for that, I fear. Proceed, directly.

CINNA: Directly, I am going to Caesar's funeral.

FIRST PLEBEIAN: As a friend or an enemy?

CINNA: As a friend.

SECOND PLEBEIAN: The matter is answered directly.

FOURTH PLEBEIAN: For your dwelling, briefly.

CINNA: Briefly, I dwell by the Capitol.

THIRD PLEBEIAN: Your name, sir, truly.

CINNA: Truly, my name is Cinna.

FIRST PLEBEIAN: Tear him to pieces! He's a conspirator.

CINNA: I am Cinna the poet, I am Cinna the poet.

FOURTH PLEBEIAN: Tear him for his bad verses, tear him for his bad verses.

CINNA: I am not Cinna the conspirator.

FOURTH PLEBEIAN: It is no matter, his name's Cinna; pluck but his name out of his heart, and turn him going.

THIRD PLEBEIAN: Tear him, tear him! Come, brands, ho! fire-brands! To Brutus', to Cassius'; burn all! Some to Decius' house, and some to Casca's; some to Ligarius'! Away go!

Further reading

All the syllabuses for English and English Literature GCSE stress the importance of wide reading. Some of your coursework must provide evidence of this. The reading that you do will help you to understand and write about the work you are going to concentrate on. The frequency and breadth of the reading will prepare you for coursework which may have to be done in controlled conditions – like a traditional examination. This will sometimes require a response to writing which has been chosen because it is likely to be unfamiliar to you, and which therefore will give your examiner a good idea of what you have really understood for yourself of what you have read. Making use of the following list, on a regular basis, is an indispensable part of preparation for GCSE. The list reflects the recommendations of the examination groups responsible for syllabuses.

Serjeant Musgrave's Dance John Arden

Consider the way the atmosphere of this play is built up. Tell the story of the arrival of the recruiting serjeant and his men in the mining village, and the effect that this has upon the colliers, and on characters like Annie and the Mayor. What is the point of the striking differences in the individual characters of the soldiers? Write about the use of music and song in a play such as this. What issues does the play force us to consider?

A Man for All Seasons Robert Bolt

What is the title suggesting? What are the pressures confronting More and what are his reactions to them? Does the play have any contemporary relevance?

Hobson's Choice Harold Brighouse

The title of this play has passed into the language. Why? Which characters do you sympathize with, and why, and at what points in the play? Do you find that your sympathies alter as the play progresses? You will probably pay most attention to Maggie, Hobson and Willie, but try not to confine your discussion to the central characters only.

A Taste of Honey Shelagh Delaney

What do you find moving about the situation and the characters of the play? Write about the dramatist's use of setting and dialogue, and the intention you think might be behind this.

The Fire Raisers Max Frisch

How does the play create a sense of menace, and in what ways does the story it tells describe the experiences of individuals and societies?

Death of a Salesman Arthur Miller

Consider the ways in which the play is humorous and also tragic. What are the dreams of the characters, and what have been the realities of their lives? What, if anything, do you find unusual or particularly striking about this play? How does the drama use shifts of time and place to dramatize aspects of the characters' inner lives?

Look Back in Anger John Osborne

What is Jimmy Porter angry about? How does the playwright use domestic scenes and what appears to be ordinary conversation to create tension between the characters and reveal their natures? Look closely at some of Jimmy's speeches – at what he is talking about and the way that he chooses to express his feelings. What gives the speeches their special force and interest? What is the importance of the play's other characters, and what interest might an audience have in them?

The Caretaker Harold Pinter

Describe the characters, setting and dialogue of the play, and say what you feel is its dramatic interest. What difficulties might the play present to a producer, and what aspects of it would you expect him to try and emphasize?

An Inspector Calls J. B. Priestley

Describe the principal characters and explain how each of them was involved in some way with the life and death of the girl. Which of the characters are changed by their experiences, and what are the attitudes of those who are not? In what ways do you find the play a realistic drama and in what ways is it a fantasy? Which speeches in the play do you think are the most important, and why?

The Dragon Eugene Schwartz

What does the play have to say about people's political behaviour? What are the difficulties and the opportunities for actors and for a producer in putting on a play like this one?

Julius Caesar Shakespeare

What are the different motives of the conspirators? What are the political tensions in the city and in what ways are they conflicts which might be experienced by other societies? What is the importance of Mark Antony and of Brutus? Look at some scenes in which the ordinary people of Rome appear. Write a diary re-ordering the events of the play as they might be viewed by such a person.

The Merchant of Venice Shakespeare

Describe the scene that you feel is the climax of the play. What is at stake at this point in the drama, and how is the conflict resolved? What are your reactions to various characters at this time?

A Midsummer Night's Dream Shakespeare

Write about the play's several stories and their common subject – love. Give a detailed account of a production that you have seen.

Which characters in the play do you think are the most important, and why? Write out some of the most memorable lines and speeches and say what you think gives them their effect.

Twelfth Night Shakespeare

Which character(s) do you find that you sympathize with, and why? Do you think that an audience is likely to admire any of the characters in the play? Give reasons for your choice. Describe in detail one scene that you think is funny. As you do so, point out whether it is character, situation, the verse itself, a combination of these elements, or something else altogether that makes for the special effect of the scene.

Androcles and the Lion Shaw

Why is this fable so appealing? What serious points do you think Shaw is making?

Journey's End R. C. Sherriff

How do the main characters illustrate different reactions to the conditions in which they find themselves? How does the dramatist make the audience feel something of the reality of the life the men were forced to lead? Write your feelings about what you think are the important scenes, and in particular about the end of the play.

The Real Inspector Hound Tom Stoppard

In what ways is this a play about plays? If you have seen a performance, or acted in one, write about the experience.

Under Milk Wood Dylan Thomas

Which characters have you found entertaining and which lines memorable? What impression of Llareggub are you left with after reading or listening to the play?

The Importance of Being Earnest Oscar Wilde

Write a clear account of the plot, as briefly as you can. What are the distinctive traits of each of the principal characters? What seem to be the targets of the writer's humour? Is it possible to take anything in the play seriously?

Poetry

Reading a poem

Poetry is language compressed and intensified so that suggestions and allusions echo in the receptive mind, rather like the effect of a stone that is thrown into still waters. The reader has to train himself to be aware of the complexity and subtlety of linguistic operation. There is no point pretending that this will come about by some automatic process, without effort on your part, or that it can be acquired by memorizing a few technical terms and applying them crudely and laboriously to the literature studied. A work of art can be read (or experienced e.g. with the performance of a play or a piece of music) many, many times before being deeply appreciated. It is in some degree an indication of the quality of an artistic creation of any kind that regularity and even frequency of experience of it is rewarding. Anything which can be fully understood and appreciated on slight acquaintance is not likely to be worth much. Apply this test to a book, play, film, or a piece of music that you have found easy to understand and like, and that you know is rather undemanding, and in honesty you would not value particularly highly: how often could you bear to read (see, hear) it before becoming impatient or bored by it? Poetry is sometimes immediately comprehensible and appealing, and sometimes the meaning has to be unravelled. Patience and effort may be required. The reader who reads only what is instantly clear and entertaining is denying himself the opportunity of exercising his mind and acquiring the more subtle perception that comes with experience of the medium. If you want your coursework to reflect a high standard of interest and commitment, then you must read regularly as part of your course, whether or not you intend to write about what you have been reading. The coursework is a sample of the work that has been done; and it will be apparent from what you have to say about the poetry that you do choose to write about, that this is not the only literature you have read. Most candidates read little poetry as part of their course – because only a third (or less) of the course may involve the study of poetry; and because they are not willing to read poetry for themselves outside formal class time. It is worth acknowledging the truth – whatever it may be – of the breadth and depth of your experience of reading poetry. It may then be perfectly possible to organize your work so that some wider reading of poetry becomes a regular part of your preparation. Use the reading list (p.89).

When you are studying a particular poem, read and re-read it. Make notes on what you have become aware of. At this stage do not worry about giving your notes any shape. Just note your impressions rapidly and freely, as they occur. Sometimes these may seem to be confused, or barely relevant. This does not matter. Do not use sentences and paragraphs yet. Simply make rough notes as you would if you were noting the important points of a passage you were going to analyse – as you might do in English, or indeed in almost any other subject. Space the notes out clearly so that they will be comprehensible to you later. It is worth practising this, to develop your skill and confidence and in any case it is a useful discipline which can be applied to other subjects.

Listen to the poem with your inner ear, so that you are aware of the sounds, rhythms and intonation of the unique 'voice' of the poem – which may be the 'voice' of the poet himself, speaking to you, as it were, or may be a voice assumed for effect.

See the patterns apparent on the page; how does the actual physical layout of the poem guide your sense of structure – the way it is built up in lines and stanzas? Many poems are of a freer and more irregular composition than prose (ordinary sentences and paragraphs); many are much more tightly, rigidly put together, with rhyme and rhythm; most poetry (like prose) still indicates meaning and connection through conventional (ordinary, normal) punctuation. To help you to understand the narrative and implied (suggested) content of a poem, think of the sentence as the primary unit of meaning, and take one sentence at a time. Do not simply read the poem line by line. Look for sentences that cross line and sometimes stanza divisions. And remember that poetry achieves much of its impact by altering the normal, expected word order within sentences; so you may have to be careful to see that you have made the right links between key words and the phrases they modify.

Once you have grasped the basic meaning of the individual sentences, you will be able to respond more securely to the interrelationship between the content of the poem and the particular form it takes:

content – story possibly; what actually happens in the poem,
      ideas contained in it or suggested by it,
      themes suggested or developed,
      the argument of the poem (the line of discussion or
      persuasion);

form   – patterns of sound and rhythm, i.e. rhyme-scheme,
      assonance, alliteration, and metre,
      structure of lines and stanzas,
      visual patterning that works to complement sound,
      syntactical structure (how the sentences are formed),
      diction (the writer's choice of words),
      imagery,
      mood, or tone,
      the narrative 'voice'.

Such subdivisions are ways of simplifying and isolating aspects of technique which make a distinctive contribution to what is one artistic whole – the poem. In the end, content and form are inseparable; one cannot exist without the other. So be careful that when you are writing about the poem, using the notes you have made on all that has occurred to you about what the poem says and how it works, you convey your understanding and appreciation of the whole. There is no point in remarking on the existence of a rhyme-scheme, or the fact that the stanzas are a certain length, or that figures of speech such as metaphor and simile are evident, unless you can say what they are doing; what they are there for, and what effect they have on the reader.

Different modes of coursework assignment

Here is a range of assignments suitable for inclusion in a GCSE coursework file for English or English Literature. The pattern reflects the move away from traditional essays towards a less rehearsed and more personal and imaginative response. The style of some of the 'open-ended' questions has received encouragement recently, but it may be judged by some teachers and examiners to have too little literary content to be satisfactory as coursework for English Literature GCSE. Caution in the framing of questions is advisable. Remember the importance of having a final folder of work that is balanced, and does not contain slight, trivial or experimental pieces at the expense of more substantial ones. Notes are provided in order to help you to appreciate the possibilities of the various forms of assignment which might be set.

The treatment of poems chosen here should be used by you as a guide to the treatment of any poems you are studying. The examples discussed in detail are limited to particular poets so that you can discover links, associations and contrasts within the material and so understand it in greater depth. You will need to read in support of these notes, and in this way the demands and the potential of some of the approaches to coursework may become clear.

Traditional structured questions

Here are examples of traditional structured questions that demand detailed knowledge and close reading. The questions within this type of exercise tend to be of increasing difficulty. They frequently begin by focusing the student's attention on the meaning of particular words and phrases, gradually widening the range of interest to the implications of certain lines/stanzas, requiring recognition and appreciation of features of style; and finally require a searching examination of aspects of the poem – that is, comment supported by reference and quotation. Within the necessarily limited focus of the question, this means:

comment – observation on the content and form of the poem, presentation of principal ideas or feelings, judgement/evaluation, personal response;

reference – referring in your own words to a word/phrase/line/ stanza/feature so as to make clear what you mean by the above, and amplified by

quotation – selecting quotation to support/prove/illustrate, e.g. brief quotations in the flow of the sentence, longer quotations introduced by the sentence, and linking/explanatory comment.

A series of short answers to such questions will not normally be acceptable as coursework. The candidate is expected to offer evidence of study in depth. It is advisable to answer the questions fully, where appropriate. Indeed, it is perfectly possible to use the questions as a series of suggestions, or starting-points, for writing – allowing the questions to determine the paragraphing and therefore provide the framework for a continuous composition.

'Death of a Naturalist'

All year the flax-dam festered in the heart
Of the townland; green and heavy-headed
Flax had rotted there, weighted down by huge sods.
Daily it sweltered in the punishing sun.
Bubbles gargled delicately, bluebottles
Wove a strong gauze of sound around the smell.
There were dragon-flies, spotted butterflies,
But best of all was the warm thick slobber
Of frogspawn that grew like clotted water
In the shade of the banks. Here, every spring
I would fill jampotfuls of the jellied
Specks to range on window-sills at home,
On shelves at school, and wait and watch until
The fattening dots burst into nimble-
Swimming tadpoles. Miss Walls would tell us how
The daddy frog was called a bullfrog
And how he croaked and how the mammy frog
Laid hundreds of little eggs and this was
Frogspawn. You could tell the weather by frogs too
For they were yellow in the sun and brown
In rain.
    Then one hot day when fields were rank
With cowdung in the grass and angry frogs
Invaded the flax-dam; I ducked through hedges
To a coarse croaking that I had not heard
Before. The air was thick with a bass chorus.
Right down the dam gross-bellied frogs were cocked
On sods; their loose necks pulsed like sails. Some hopped:
The slap and plop were obscene threats. Some sat
Poised like mud grenades, their blunt heads farting.
I sickened, turned, and ran. The great slime kings
Were gathered there for vengeance and I knew
That if I dipped my hand the spawn would clutch it.

Seamus Heaney

Assignment

1 Comment on the poet's use of: 'festered'; 'delicately'; 'gauze'.

2 How would you describe the tone of the lines alluding to Miss Walls?

3 Can you detect a change of rhythmic emphasis in the second stanza? What effect does it have?

4 Comment, using reference and quotation, on the change in the attitude of the persona or 'voice' of the poem.

Notes

The accurate, realistic description conveys the immediacy of an experience. The figurative language is forceful and clear, and contributes to the reader's perception; its purpose is not merely ornamental. Similarly, the rhythms of the poem register changes of mood. The writing is a sensuous exploration of the origin of feeling in memory and in experience, and the poem modifies this memory by arrangements of words in forms that suit what it is the writer has to say; this is the artifice, or workmanship, that makes art of the perceptions of experience. To the child the 'self' is unknown; the adult, reflective mind explores the development of a conscious self or personality through an examination of fragments of memory such as we all have – that remain, whether invited or not. They sometimes possess or acquire a meaning which is recognized, although barely understood at the time, perhaps, and which can only be retrieved in the recollection and consideration of maturity. The poem tells a story, and, like many poems that are sophisticated as well as direct, it may be understood on several different levels. The strands of meaning are unravelled and draw the reader into the dark centre of the poet's past, and perhaps they also inspire reflection. In a sense, the experience that the writer re-creates is the universal one in which appearances are discovered to have been illusory.

The words pointed out in the first question direct the reader's attention to the physical texture of the scene; they are among the many appeals the poet makes to the senses, giving a lush, over-ripe quality to the writing that conveys a primitive relish for slime and buzzing flies, the fertile decomposition that the 'Naturalist' loves. The cosy, simplifying humanity of Miss Walls, the teacher, is evoked by the poem ironically adopting her language. The tone becomes that of the well-meaning, patronizing schoolmarm who gingerly touches the seeds of generation – unconsciously tidying away mystery before the child's innocent, receptive mind can get to work on it. The rhythm of the second stanza strengthens the gravity of blank verse by making the beat slower and more weighty, suggesting jerky yet ponderous movement:

> ... gross-bellied frogs were cocked
> On sods; their loose necks pulsed like sails. Some hopped

The enthusiasm and security of the first stanza can be illustrated by references to the scene itself, the profusion of life incubating in the flax-dam, and the annual ritual of collection and explanation. The second stanza gives us anger and invasion, and fear of the unknown. The boy runs from the creatures, the 'great slime kings' who have come to avenge his presumptuous interference in the primeval world. This is the moment when life precipitates the boy from protected childhood into the uncertainty of adolescence. The reassuring stability of things is no more, and the boy has had a glimpse of shadows he had never imagined, and from which, now, he will never be entirely free. The poem re-creates an instant of perception that marks the inescapable transition from the child's sense of the world as finite and rooted in place, relationship and significance, to an awareness of the submerged threat in the revelations of experience. The adolescent exists in a dynamic, pulsating, ominously physical state in which nothing – not even the most familiar and comforting rituals of home and school – may be taken at face value.

'The Darkling Thrush'

I leant upon a coppice gate
    When Frost was spectre-gray,
And Winter's dregs made desolate
    The weakening eye of day.
The tangled bine-stems scored the sky
    Like strings of broken lyres,
And all mankind that haunted nigh
    Had sought their household fires.

The land's sharp features seemed to be
   The Century's corpse outleant,
His crypt the cloudy canopy,
   The wind his death-lament.
The ancient pulse of germ and birth
   Was shrunken hard and dry,
And every spirit upon the earth
   Seemed fervourless as I.

At once a voice arose among
   The bleak twigs overhead
In a full-hearted evensong
   Of joy illimited;
An aged thrush, frail, gaunt, and small,
   In blast-beruffled plume,
Had chosen thus to fling his soul
   Upon the growing gloom.

So little cause for carolings
   Of such ecstatic sound
Was written on terrestrial things
   Afar or nigh around,
That I could think there trembled through
   His happy good-night air
Some blessed Hope, whereof he knew
   And I was unaware.

Thomas Hardy
31 December 1900

Assignment

1 (a) Imagine that you are the poet. Drawing your information from the first two stanzas only, write about what you see as you lean on the gate, and the mood which this inspires in you.
(b) Comment on the following: 'spectre-gray'; 'the weakening eye of day'; 'the Century's corpse'.

2 (a) What change of mood takes place in the last two stanzas? What causes this change?
(b) Comment on the following and show their importance to the understanding of the poem: 'in a full-hearted evensong'; 'to fling his soul'; 'ecstatic sound'; 'some blessed Hope'.

Notes

Be careful to leave nothing out. What is the season? The time of day? Quote from the text to show where the information comes from. It is a cold day in winter, and the land is in the grip of frost; the mood is one of sadness, the time of year and the scenery suggest death and decay to the poet; the frost is ghostly – 'spectre-gray', and the effect of winter on the landscape – 'Winter's dregs', presumably bare boughs, the absence of crops and flowers, is to make it 'desolate'. It is late afternoon, for the light is fading; this is referred to as 'the weakening eye of day', which contributes to the sense of a failing of vigour. What objects does the poet see? He mentions only a climbing hedge-row plant, not reduced to a meaningless tangle of dead and dry stems, which, seen against the light, remind him of the broken strings of a musical instrument; again the image is one of destruction. The land is deserted – everyone is indoors, seeking warmth. Is the mood continued in the second stanza? The mood is intensified, and it is death particularly which is in the poet's mind. The earth is seen as a 'corpse', the sky – the 'cloudy canopy' – as the roof of its burial place, the wind sings a song of mourning; all life-giving impulse has stopped, is 'shrunken hard and dry'. The poet sees the whole world as sharing his own lack of animation, or 'fervour'.

Explain what the phrases mean, then consider in what ways they contribute to the poem. 'Spectre-gray' means grey, like a ghost. It is both a literal description of the colour of the frost, and suggests the silence and deadliness of its power. 'The weakening eye of day' refers to the fading light. The use of the word 'weakening', and the personification of the sun's light make us feel that the sun, the source of life, is failing, and this contributes to the atmosphere of decay and death, present in the opening of the poem. The date at the end of the poem tells us what we might otherwise guess: that the poem is written at the end of the year, at the turn of the century; the poet is referring to the century which has reached its end when he speaks of 'the Century's corpse'; that the image which springs to the poet's mind to describe time past should be a dead body is in keeping with the sombre mood of the stanza.

To answer this question in sufficient detail you must read the last stanzas very carefully, and try to follow the poet's train of thought. A thrush begins to sing; the poet notices that it is old, thin and weak, suffering, no doubt, from the cold wind which ruffles its feathers. The frozen world – 'terrestrial things' – could not justify joy from any part of creation, but least of all from something as vulnerable as this poor bird. Why then is he singing with 'joy illimited'? The vocabulary shows us that the poet's mind turns to religion: the bird's song is referred to as evensong – a Church service, the fact that he sings with all his might is described as 'flings his soul'; we are told that there is no reason for his song in anything 'terrestrial' – we suppose, then, that we must look to the supernatural for its cause. The poet concludes that the bird must instinctively perceive something which is not apparent, and which is hidden from his own rational mind; he begins to hope – 'I could think', and as 'Hope' is written with a capital letter and referred to as 'blessed', we feel what the thrush perceives and the poet does not is the reality of God.

Consider what the phrases mean; could any of them have more than one meaning? Have they any associations for you? Do they suggest anything to you? 'In a full-hearted evensong' has both the sense that the bird was singing joyfully in the evening, and, bearing in mind that 'Evensong' is the name of a Church service, that the bird is praising God. 'To fling his soul' refers to the intense emotion of his song and the energy of his perform-ance; the choice of the word 'soul', taken together with the other words with religious connotations, imply a religious motive for the song. 'Ecstatic sound' means that the sound denoted intense delight, but 'ecstasy' has the sense of being transported outside one's normal self, and this would contribute to the sense of the bird's song being an act of worship, uniting it with God. 'Some blessed Hope': the term 'blessed' can mean 'happy', but is most frequently used by the Christian Church when referring to God or the saints; it is usual for Christians to begin any term which means 'God' with a capital letter. Here we understand that the poet's hope is that God exists, perceived by the thrush, although not yet by himself.

'Thistles'

Against the rubber tongues of cows and the hoeing hands of men
Thistles spike the summer air
Or crackle open under a blue-black pressure.

Every one a revengeful burst
Of resurrection, a grasped fistful
Of splintered weapons and Icelandic frost thrust up

From the underground stain of a decayed Viking.
They are like pale hair and the gutturals of dialects.
Every one manages a plume of blood.

Then they grow grey, like men.
Mown down, it is a feud. Their sons appear
Stiff with weapons, fighting back over the same ground.

Ted Hughes

Assignment

1 Why has the poet chosen the word 'rubber' to describe the cows' tongues?

2 Explain what is happening in lines 2 and 3.

3 What is the thistle seen as in lines 4–7?

4 Which words in these lines actually describe the thistle?

5 The thistle is seen as having a purpose in growing. Which word tells us this.

6 Give two words from these lines which indicate energetic purpose.

7 What does 'a plume of blood' refer to?

8 Which part of the thistle's life-cycle is described in the first line of the last stanza?

9 What is the poet describing in the last stanza? Why does he say 'it is a feud'?

10 What do you find unusual or striking about the poem, in the images created or in the overall suggestion of the poem?

Notes

The countryside that is so easily taken for granted – as if it has always been there in the form that we inherit – is the record of man's endeavour, for good or ill, and the poem is a kind of hymn to the violent energy at the powerful core of the cycle of nature. The unwanted flowers are wreaths on the unmarked graves of dead warriors. The thistle becomes a metaphor for the indestructible heroism of the marauder. Men die, but the memory of their lives and the effects of their actions are never erased.

The poet begins by describing the thistle growing – 'spike the summer air', and its flower – 'a blue-black pressure' bursting through the sepals. They continue to grow, despite their enemies – men trying to get rid of them by hoeing, and cows who eat them; they are so spiky that the cows' tongues are described as 'rubber' by the poet, to indicate their insensitivity.

Imagine that they have sprung from the corpse of a long-buried Viking. The poet first sees them as his weapons, which have 'splintered' into the many tiny sharp points which make up a thistle leaf and are touched with 'Icelandic frost' – presumably the small hairs on the leaf, which create a whitish sheen. Their intentions are 'revengeful', the energy of their purpose described in the words 'burst' and 'thrust up'. Their flower is referred to as 'a plume of blood'.

In the last stanza their seed-time is described. 'Grow grey' refers to the downy seeds which now replace the flower. If, at this point, they are cut down, the seeds scatter and grow again the following year, as if they were sons avenging their fathers' deaths, engaged in 'a feud' with man.

The compelling tone created by slow, staccato lines, keeps the reader at a distance from the natural scene and makes an ordinary working field into a surrealistic collage of warning, bleeding flowers that refuse to die. Here the poet is an observer and interpreter, not a judge. The past is illuminated in the mystery of the present, and we have a partial understanding, both of how things are and how they came to be, in this fragmentary glimpse of the interconnecting facts of life and death.

'Plain texts' questions

Here are some examples of assignments in which the emphasis is on the ability to discuss the detail of the poem. The 'open book' or 'plain texts' examinations that have encouraged this type of assignment have sought to reward the candidate who can make sense of the text when it is put in front of him, and who does not depend on recall or a rehearsed approach. The candidate's writing can be more spontaneous and creative, and a genuine response can be developed. The questions sometimes ask for commentary and appreciation:

commentary – this means going carefully through the poem, noting content, form, and the writer's intentions,

appreciation – how successful these prove to be, and what your own reactions to the work are.

Sometimes the questions are deliberately directed, and your attention is focused on particular aspects – the imagery of a poem, for example, or the effect of its sounds and rhythms. The expectation is that the argument you construct will be soundly based on what is presented to you, or on what you are asked to read.

Here is an example of an exercise that demands comment and interpretation. Read the following poem by Robert Frost.

'The Road not Taken'

Two roads diverged in a yellow wood,
And sorry I could not travel both
And be one traveller, long I stood
And looked down one as far as I could
To where it bent in the undergrowth;

Then took the other, as just as fair,
And having perhaps the better claim,
Because it was grassy and wanted wear;
Though as for that the passing there
Had worn them really about the same,

And both that morning equally lay
In leaves no step had trodden black.
Oh, I kept the first for another day!
Yet knowing how way leads on to way,
I doubted if I should ever come back.

I shall be telling this with a sigh
Somewhere ages and ages hence:
Two roads diverged in a yellow wood, and I –
I took the one less travelled by,
And that has made all the difference.

Robert Frost

Assignment

1 Write what you think actually happens in the poem.

2 Explain the feelings the poet expresses in the lines:
Oh, I kept the first for another day!
Yet knowing how way leads to way,
I doubted if I should ever come back.

3 What do you think that the poet is suggesting in the last verse of the poem?

Notes

This exercise offers an opportunity to reveal an understanding of a poem that goes beyond a literal re-statement of surface meaning. The first question directs attention to the paths, the season, the thoughtful traveller, and the unavoidable necessity of choice. A perfectly satisfactory answer to this part of the task might simply stick to the idea of the journey and the paths that cannot both be taken at the same time; and, in other words, tell the story of the poem.

The second and third questions encourage you to consider the deeper, underlying meaning of the poem – the idea that life is full of paths, choices that have to be made, sometimes without there being any obvious reason for one decision rather than another. The poet recognizes the natural feeling that one can always retrace steps, but he is wise enough to admit reluctantly to himself that in all probability he will never return; after all, 'way leads on to way': one road leads on to another. What has 'made all the difference' to his life (and to everybody's?) is the drift into a decision to take one opportunity that presented itself, rather than to wait for – or make – another. Perhaps the 'voice' of the poem is suggesting that we are all prisoners of accident. What do you sense the tone of the poem to be: wistful, sad, melancholy, resigned, philosophical? Give reasons for your conclusion, and refer closely to the text in support of it.

Assignment

Show how 'Death of a Naturalist' (see p.55) is a simple, narrative poem of childhood experience, which is also richly evocative of scene, and which closes dramatically with a grotesque image of the end of innocence.

Notes

The assignment provides the structure or plan for the piece of coursework. The first requirement is that you should literally tell the story of the poem, bringing out what you think is important about what the first-person narrator feels about what happened to him. Mention his sheer enjoyment of what he saw as the natural world, and his confident sense of understanding it. On one level then, the poem initially works as a nostalgic memory of the enclosure of youth. The clotted, gargling, spawning of life is a kind of music to him. The first four sentences of the poem concentrate on making the flax-dam as real to us as possible. We see it, heavy in the 'heart of the townland', feel the heat of the 'sweltering sun', hear the delicate bubbling accompanied by the buzz of the 'gauze' woven around the smell. We can almost touch the 'thick slobber/Of frogspawn' for ourselves.

The climax of the poem is the assault of the seething, croaking, farting instruments of vengeance. In the second stanza the appeal to the senses is made in terms of the child's terror at the inexplicable darkness and menace that has erupted from the familiar. The revolting physicality of the experience carries suggestions of the child's unconscious response to the changes that occur in his own physical being with dawning sexuality: the air is thick, the frogs 'gross-bellied', the slapping and plopping is 'obscene', and the blunt-headed creatures are 'mud grenades', explosive with fertility. The frogs are real enough; but the image of them as 'slime kings' is a powerful distortion that conveys the stunning shock of realization. What is it that has ended?

'Ambulances'

Closed like confessionals, they thread
Loud noons of cities, giving back
None of the glances they absorb.
Light glossy grey, arms on a plaque,
They come to rest at any kerb:
All streets in time are visited.

Then children strewn on steps or road,

Or women coming from the shops
Past smells of different dinners, see
A wild white face that overtops
Red stretcher-blankets momently
As it is carried in and stowed,

And sense the solving emptiness
That lies just under all we do,
And for a second get it whole,
So permanent and blank and true.
The fastened doors recede. *Poor soul*,
They whisper at their own distress;

For borne away in deadened air
May go the sudden shut of loss
Round something nearly at an end,
And what cohered in it across
The years, the unique random blend
Of families and fashions, there

At last begin to loosen. Far
From the exchange of love to lie
Unreachable inside a room
The traffic parts to let go by
Brings closer what is left to come,
And dulls to distance all we are.

Philip Larkin

Assignment

Write a commentary and appreciation of 'Ambulances'.

Notes

How does the poet convey the secrecy of what happens in the ambulance? Consider the word 'confessionals', to which ambulances are likened; these are places in Roman Catholic churches where a penitent tells his sins, in secret, to a priest, who may never reveal what he has heard. Look at the phrase 'giving back/None of the glances they absorb'; everyone stares curiously at the ambulance, but those inside looking out cannot be seen by them, because the windows are made of darkened glass. What feeling is evoked by the last two lines of the first stanza? We feel uneasy, perhaps afraid. 'At any kerb' suggests the way in which misfortune strikes haphazardly; 'all streets in time are visited' reminds us that death is eventually the lot of everyone, and that, although we have escaped this time, our turn will inevitably come.

In stanzas two and three, two aspects of life are contrasted. How does the poet convey the ordinary facts of everyday life? What breaks this smooth surface and causes a momentary perception of something deeper? At the beginning of the second stanza everyday life is presented through a street scene; the daily routine of shopping and cooking is taking place, but is suddenly interrupted by the removal of a person, presumably from a house, into an ambulance, which, for a moment, shatters the trivial pattern of daily existence. What does the poet mean by 'the solving emptiness/That lies just under all we do'? Why, in our busy lives, do we usually not 'get it whole'? Whom do the housewives pity, besides the person in the ambulance? The knowledge that we must die, 'so permanent and blank and true', is not in the forefront of our minds as we go about our daily business, but we are aware of it 'just under all we do'; the sight of the ambulance momentarily focuses our whole attention on it. Death, 'emptiness', is the final solution of all our problems, and the awareness of death solves them on a day-to-day basis by making us aware of their essential unimportance. The women whisper 'Poor soul' about the neighbour in the ambulance, but their 'distress' is occasioned by the awareness that it will, at some time, be their turn to be taken away.

Where is the 'deadened air', mentioned in the first line of the fourth stanza? Why is 'deadened' a good choice of word? What does it convey to you? 'May go the sudden shut of loss' is a very evocative line; try to explain exactly why. What is the poet referring to by 'something nearly at an end'? Can you explain in a word or short phrase what is meant by 'what cohered in it across/The years, the unique random blend/Of families and fashions'? The air is 'deadened' because the tightly-shut ambulance door keeps out all disturbance; like the patient, it is cut off from everyday life. This detail contributes to the sense of isolation which this stanza depicts. The word 'shut' in the second line suggests the literal shutting of the ambulance door, but also the patient's isolation, for, as that door shuts, he is severed from his normal life, and separated, perhaps for ever, from everything that is familiar; he experiences distress, caused by his sense of this 'loss'. The use of the word 'something' for the person whose life is 'nearly at an end' has the effect of distancing the person, and conveys the poet's dread of his condition – if he is seen as a person, like us, we identify with him, which is painful, and are forced to acknowledge that what is about to happen to him – death – will also inevitably happen to us. The final three lines of the stanza refer to the human personality, which is composed of a 'random blend' of inherited characteristics – 'families', and the ideas current during a lifetime – 'fashions'; because of the manner of its formation, it is without duplicate, 'unique', and in the use of this word we feel the poet's sense of the wonder of human life.

What are we told, in the last stanza, about the effect of the sudden removal on the patient? Why does the poet say 'begin to loosen'? In the lines 'Far/From the exchange of love to lie/ Unreachable' we are shown a moving and frightening picture of isolation. What is necessary for the 'exchange of love', which the person in the ambulance is denied? The person is seen as being at the end of his life; what, then, is left to come? The patient is separated from his loved ones, and his sense of deprivation and the desperate feeling that he can do nothing about it, that he is 'unreachable', is vividly evoked by these lines. The only reality left is his approaching death – 'what is left to come' – which is brought 'closer' by the stress of 'loss'; his personality, 'what cohered . . . across the years', is breaking up – begins 'to loosen', and we feel life ebbing away in the phrase 'dulls to distance all we are'.

'Anthem for Doomed Youth'

What passing-bells for these who die as cattle?
    Only the monstrous anger of the guns.
    Only the stuttering rifles' rapid rattle
Can patter out their hasty orisons.
No mockeries now for them; no prayers nor bells;
    Nor any voice of mourning save the choirs, –
The shrill, demented choirs of wailing shells;
    And bugles calling for them from sad shires.

What candles may be held to speed them all?
    Not in the hands of boys but in their eyes
Shall shine the holy glimmers of good-byes.
    The pallor of girls' brows shall be their pall;

Their flowers the tenderness of patient minds,
And each slow dusk a drawing-down of blinds.

Wilfred Owen

Assignment

Owen is comparing the circumstances surrounding death on the battlefield with those surrounding death at home. Write about what you think is important in the poem.

Notes

Owen makes the point of the poem in the striking first line: war does not mean glory, the individual magnified – but depersonalization, man is reduced to being a number, one of a herd, nothing more than an animal, driven to death as cattle to slaughter.

He develops this idea throughout the poem, detailing the civilian ceremonies: the church bell – 'passing-bell' – tolling to tell the parish that someone has died, the prayers – 'orisons' – for the dead man's soul, the choirs singing hymns; the respect shown for the corpse, placed in a coffin covered by a cloth – 'pall' – and surrounded by candles, and tributes of flowers; the closing of curtains in the dead man's house to signify mourning. These ceremonies imply respect for each individual; they are part of the Christian burial rites, and bring to our minds the beliefs of this religion – that man is made in the image of a God who is interested in the fate of each individual. This contrasts with what is happening at the front, where death is wholesale and without any dignifying ritual, and emphasizes the degradation of war.

Words carry suggestions, indirect as well as direct meanings. Sometimes their sound itself creates a picture. The first stanza shows the violence of the front. The phrase 'monstrous anger' does more than describe the noise of the guns – it evokes fear; the personification of the guns, and the use of the word 'monstrous' give the impression of something superhuman, whose 'anger' is correspondingly greater than man is capable of, and we have an instant perception of them as a terrifying power, dealing out death on a frightening scale. The nature of rifle fire is vividly and economically conveyed by the onomatopoeia (word suggesting sound) of 'stuttering', 'rapid', 'rattle' and 'patter', and the alliteration (repetition of initial letter) in 'rifles' rapid rattle'. In the line 'The shrill, demented choirs of wailing shells', the words 'shrill' and 'wailing' convey so clearly the trajectory of the shells that we immediately visualize a battlefield; 'demented' aptly describes Owen's view of their purpose; these words can also describe the effect of grief on the human voice and mind, and superimposed on the fighting we see mourners singing a funeral dirge.

This is an 'anthem' – a hymn – and the tone is dignified and sombre. In the first stanza the violence is present in the structure, but in a controlled and measured way. The opening line is set in the form of a question, beginning innocently enough, with the shock in the unexpectedness of the last word, whose very sound is cutting. The form of question and answer, the onomatopoeia, the staccato effect produced by the short phrases and heavy stops of 'No mockeries now for them; no prayers nor bells;' gives a troubled rhythm, which contributes to the indignant anger of the verse. In the second the dominant mood is sadness, and the rhythm is measured. The lines flow unbroken, stopped only at the ends; the sounds are soft, there is nothing staccato; the use of alliteration and the repetition of similar vowel sounds lengthen the lines and contribute to the elegiac nature of the poem:

'Shall shine the holy glimmer of good-byes'
'The pallor of girls' brows shall be their pall'
'And each slow dusk a drawing-down of blinds.'

'Open-ended' questions

Here are some examples of assignments that illustrate a more open-ended approach to a piece of writing. The poem is regarded as a catalyst – a starting-point, or stimulus – to which the reader brings life and meaning.

Here, the emphasis is on originality and vitality of response, and there is greater freedom to develop ideas. With coursework intended specifically for the English Literature file, it should be remembered that responses ought to be firmly rooted in the text – that is, your reader must be able to see as clearly the connection between the poem and the writing as you do, and indeed it

must be made clear that the content and quality of your writing
have depended upon an initial reading.

'Dulce Et Decorum Est'

Bent double, like old beggars under sacks,
Knock-kneed, coughing like hags, we cursed through sludge,
Till on the haunting flares we turned our backs
And towards our distant rest began to trudge.
Men marched asleep. Many had lost their boots
But limped on, blood-shod. All went lame; all blind;
Drunk with fatigue; deaf even to the hoots
Of tired, outstripped Five-Nines that dropped behind.

Gas! Gas! Quick, boys! – An ecstasy of fumbling,
Fitting the clumsy helmets just in time;
But someone still was yelling out and stumbling,
And flound'ring like a man in fire or lime . . .
Dim, through the misty panes and thick green light,
As under a green sea, I saw him drowning.

In all my dreams, before my helpless sight,
He plunges at me, guttering, choking, drowning.

If in some smothering dreams you too could pace
Behind the wagon that we flung him in,
And watch the white eyes writhing in his face,
His hanging face, like a devil's sick of sin;
If you could hear, at every jolt, the blood
Come gargling from the froth-corrupted lungs,
Obscene as cancer, bitter as the cud
Of vile, incurable sores on innocent tongues, –
My friend, you would not tell with such high zest
To children ardent for some desperate glory,
The old Lie: Dulce et decorum est
Pro patria mori.

Wilfred Owen

Assignment

What is this poem saying to us? What is your response to it?

Notes

Owen was writing about the First World War – the war to end

war, as some thought at the time – in which a generation of young volunteers died in conditions of mechanized mass-destruction. The title of this poem is part of the quotation given in full in the last line. This is from the Latin poet, Horace, and means that it is a pleasant and fitting thing to die for your country. Owen sets out a violently opposed view of sacrifice – in which it is life that is sacred, not an abstract notion of the fatherland.

Having read the title, we turn to the first stanza expecting the conventional picture of proud and efficient young warriors; it is with a sense of shock that we read this description of men who are seen as 'old beggars', who 'cough', 'trudge', 'curse', 'limp', so 'drunk with fatigue' that they are not aware of the gas attack. Youth is destroyed in a landscape from hell. There is neither honour nor glory here.

In the horrifying description which follows, someone fails to get his gas mask on in time, and the poet observes the effect of the gas on a human being – 'I saw him drowning'. The horror is so intense that the scene haunts the poet's dreams.

The soldier is taken behind the lines in a wagon, and the poet tells us that if we could experience his own 'smothering dreams' of this event we would not encourage eager children to think that war is glorious. Here we have an actual description, and comparisons which convey the poet's feelings of anger and indignation at this unmerited suffering: 'like a devil's sick of sin' and 'bitter as the cud/Of vile, incurable sores on innocent tongues'. He refers to the quotation from which the title is taken as 'The old Lie', and this insult is the culmination of the poem. Anger and compassion inspire the description; the poem does not stand back and invite the reader to consider and to judge for himself. This is an aggressive assault on the conscience of those who, in the poet's view, perpetuate the idea of honourable sacrifice by their conditioning – and therefore corruption – of the next generation. The spirit of the poem may not necessarily be unpatriotic or pacifist; it is pointing to the discrepancy between the purpose of war (which might be defence of life, territory or principle) and the means by which this is pursued (destruction of life and territory, and perhaps the setting aside of other principles?). The poet is concerned to tell the truth about the common soldier's experience of war – a stark contrast to the romantic exhortations of non-combatants.

Take the argument of the poem as a starting-point for consideration and expression of opinion. Did you agree with the poet, Horace, before reading this poem? Has reading the poem changed your views in any way? Which, in your opinion, is more likely to convince the reader of the poet's ideas: the information he is providing, or the emotion and conviction with which he presents it? Try to illustrate your initial discussion by referring back to the detail of the poem; then widen the frame of reference by considering how your own views have been formed – by direct experience of violence, terrorism or war perhaps; by the values assimilated from family and culture; and from the wealth of literature and reportage to which you have been exposed – countless poems, plays, films, novels, accounts, reports and memoirs.

Assignment

Referring to what you see as the most important features of Seamus Heaney's poem 'Death of a Naturalist' (see p.55), write about an incident in your own life in which your perception of reality has been altered so that you no longer see things in the same way. Indicate similarities and parallels between your experience and the one described in the poem.

Notes

The question asks you to keep in mind what you see as the significant elements of the poem. It is a description of a time of stability and security that disintegrates under the pressure of life unfolding, and it conveys something of the physical and emotional turbulence that means the end of childhood. The incident, harmless and innocent as it is, nonetheless reveals to the persona of the poem – the child whom we presume is now the poet – a disturbing reality hitherto unimagined. Try to use these aspects of the poem as reference points for writing that goes beyond it. It is not enough, however, to write a poem or a piece of prose that reflects only your own experience; you must also relate your understanding of your own changing perception to what you have read in the poem. Supposing that an incident does come to mind – when you discovered a fear of heights, or water; you were left alone, or were lost; a new friend or an animal became a threat; familiar surroundings assumed frightening characteristics – use the pattern of the poem to help you to put your reflections in some sort of order. Think of your early pleasure and certainty; refer to ways that this is described in the poem, and present your parallel recollections. How is the dramatic change recorded by Heaney? What descriptions and images can you create to convey the shock to your own sensibilities that your experience meant? Seamus Heaney is writing about a rural childhood of relative certainty and emotional security – the warmth and richness of the poem seem to assure the reader of this. Whilst admitting the general truth of the poet's portrayal of the fragility of understanding, you may wish to refer to experience which contrasts in some way with that of the setting of the poem. The assignment is not intended to limit your writing to the discovery of narrow similarities, it is seeking to encourage a searching consideration and illustration of themes central to the poem.

'Faintheart in a Railway Train'

At nine in the morning there passed a church,
At ten there passed me by the sea,
At twelve a town of smoke and smirch,
At two a forest of oak and birch,
   And then, on a platform, she:

A radiant stranger, who saw not me.
I said, 'Get out to her do I dare?'
But I kept my seat in my search for a plea,
And the wheels moved on. O could it but be
   That I had alighted there!

Thomas Hardy

Assignment

Imagine that you are on quite a long journey. You are looking at the scenery. What do you see? What are your feelings as time passes? You suddenly see a complete stranger to whom you are instantly attracted. What do you do? Imagine yourself searching for an excuse to approach the stranger. What are your thoughts and feelings? How did it happen that you did nothing? What exactly are your feelings about this missed opportunity, as you move on?

Notes

Notice the title, and bear it in mind as you write; remember that, basically, you fail to do what the more adventurous part of you, at least, wants to do.

Make a conscious effort to put yourself in the poet's place. Visualize the scenery, and imagine what you feel as the journey lengthens.

Make clear the suddenness of the emotion you feel on seeing the stranger. Notice the word 'radiant': try to convey the intensity of your own attraction.

You are finally not adventurous enough to make an approach. Make the reader feel the conflict between the different parts of your personality, before you reach this decision.

Try to express vividly what you feel as your journey takes you irrevocably on.

'Snow in the Suburbs'

 Every branch big with it,
 Bent every twig with it;
Every fork like a white web-foot;
Every street and pavement mute;
Some flakes have lost their way, and grope back upward, when
Meeting those meandering down they turn and descend again.
 The palings are glued together like a wall,
 And there is not waft of wind with the fleecy fall.

 A sparrow enters the tree,
 Whereon immediately
A snow-lump thrice his own slight size
Descends on him and showers his head and eyes,
 And overturns him,
 And near inurns him,
 And lights on a nether twig, when its brush
Starts off a volley of other lodging lumps with a rush.
 The steps are a blanched slope,
 Up which, with feeble hope,
A black cat comes, wide-eyed and thin;
 And we take him in.

Thomas Hardy

Assignment

Write a passage, in verse or in prose, describing an aspect of nature which has impressed you; you could choose a scene, a place at a certain time of day, a type of weather, a flower, an animal's actions, water, a field or a park in the early morning, a beach at sunset – anything which you know well and can describe in detail.

Notes

This poem is written in light-hearted mood, expressing sheer pleasure in nature. The charm of the poem lies in its detailed observation, and the delight we sense behind this. The scene is almost too perfect. The city is muffled by the gentle snowfall. Notice how the rhythm imitates the irregular fall of the snow-flakes, and how the soft sounds of the lines evoke the comforting claustrophobia of falling snow. The wry comedy of the second stanza gives us a cartoon-like picture of the sparrow tumbling in a mini-avalanche through the branches. The final image is of the forlorn cat taken in from the beautiful but inhospitable wastes by the anonymous 'we'.

The poem is a description which is part observation, part expression of pleasure, and part creation of mood. As you make notes for your own writing, record the sense-impressions made by the scene you have chosen. Your writing should build on the detail of these impressions, and the sound, rhythm and imagery of your poem or writing will grow out of your patterning or arrangement of this source material. Try to write about something or somewhere you feel strongly about, for your feelings will then be apparent in your style, and will make your work sincere and interesting. Visualize what you are going to describe. Do you know enough about the scene to describe it in detail, or can you go there again and actually record what you see, hear, feel, and smell – and all that this makes you reflect on?

'The Dead-Beat'

He dropped, – more sullenly than wearily,
Lay stupid like a cod, heavy like meat,
And none of us could kick him to his feet;
– Just blinked at my revolver, blearily;

– Didn't appear to know a war was on,
Or see the blasted trench at which he stared.
'I'll do 'em in,' he whined. 'If this hand's spared,
I'll murder them, I will.'

        A low voice said,
'It's Blighty, p'raps, he sees; his pluck's all gone,
Dreaming of the valiant, that *aren't* dead:
Bold uncles, smiling ministerially;
Maybe his brave young wife, getting her fun
In some new home, improved materially.
It's not these stiffs have crazed him; nor the Hun.'

We sent him down at last, out of the way.
Unwounded; – stout lad, too, before that strafe.
Malingering? Stretcher-bearers winked, 'Not half!'

Next day I heard the Doc's well-whiskied laugh:
'That scum you sent last night soon died. Hooray!'

Wilfred Owen

Assignment

You are the soldier, writing a letter to a friend at home to explain your position, and your thoughts and feelings, as you lie in hospital after being sent back from the front line.

Notes

Before writing, you may find it helpful to consider the following points:

Bearing in mind that Owen's generation would have been taught to think of the war as a heroic and justified defence of one's country, and fighting in it the duty of a man, whom do we suppose the soldier wishes to 'murder' at the end of the first stanza?

'Blighty' is soldiers' slang for England, home. 'Strafe', from the German *strafen*, to punish, refers here to a bombardment. It seems that the bombardment that the soldiers have just been through has been one too many for this man. Someone suggests that his condition is not directly caused, as one might think, by the physical horrors of war. What cause is suggested?

The stretcher-bearers seem to think he is malingering –

pretending to be ill; the doctor seems to think so too. Yet he died – why, do you think?

General coursework assignments

The following assignments can be adapted to suit virtually any poems you are studying. They are designed to provide written work. Some of them will require group preparation, and, if it is possible to include a record of the practical element, then this might be accepted for assessment. Tapes and video-recordings could be used to support and illustrate what you have written.

All the poems mentioned in this section can be found in the anthologies listed on pp.90–1, copies of which should be available from your school library.

1 Read, analyse, and write an appreciation of a selection of poems by one poet. What general comments is it fair to make about their subjects and the writer's special style? What similarities and differences do you note when comparing the poems? What have you found out about the poet's life and work? Is any of this relevant to the understanding of his poetry? What aspects of the writing would make you recommend, or not recommend, the poems to your fellow students?

2 Write about a selection of poems of a specific type – ballads, for example. What are their distinctive features? How various have you found the examples? Read some anonymous folk ballads from England and America, and then look at poems that employ the ballad form: for example, 'O What is That Sound' (W. H. Auden), and 'Danny Deever' (Rudyard Kipling).

3 Write an account of four or five poems which are linked by mood. They might be about love, fear, nature, sleep, or childhood, for example. In what different ways do you find the writing conveys the nature of the experience, or is moving?

4 Compare poems that are written in English but come from very distinct cultures within England or the English-speaking world. Discuss the interests and attitudes of the writing, and note what is individual or interesting about it.

5 Consider some poems that look at familiar scenes – urban or rural – in an unusual way. Look at T. S. Eliot's 'Preludes' for

example, and John Betjeman's satirical 'Harvest Hymn'.

6 Examine some poems that depend for their effect on unusual devices, visual or verbal. Look at the writings of e. e. cummings and Lawrence Ferlinghetti, for example.

7 Record a group discussion of some poems that are interesting and thought-provoking, but not immediately easy to understand:
'The Second Coming' (W. B. Yeats)
'Not Waving But Drowning' (Stevie Smith)
'Stopping by Woods on a Snowy Evening' (Robert Frost)
'Ozymandias' (Shelley)
Make a transcript of the discussion, and add further comments on the poems and what was said about them.

8 Compile an anthology of your favourite poems and write an introduction to the collection.

9 How important is rhythm to poetry? Consider some poems that are quite different in tone and intention, but nonetheless are remarkable for their dependence on rhythm:
'Tarantella' (Hilaire Belloc)
'The Tyger' (William Blake)
'Skimbleshanks: The Railway Cat' (T. S. Eliot);
or choose any two or three poems of distinctive rhythm and say what effect this has e.g. 'Night Mail' by Auden and 'Prayer Before Birth' by MacNeice.

10 Read some poems that are linked thematically – that is, they share an interest in a particular subject, although their treatment of it might be radically different. Many anthologies group poems in this way, and so it is not difficult to gather material. Here are some themes to consider: ambition; courage; fear; old age; honesty; law and order; change – and permanence, in the natural world and in the man-made one; justice, and judgement; love; conviction; loyalty; loneliness; families; occupations; conflict and stress; pleasure, and happiness; memories; the unfamiliar. Here are some suggestions for groups of poems on a single theme:

animals: 'Snake' (D. H. Lawrence)
'Death of a Pig' (Ted Hughes)
'Pike' (Edmund Blunden)

Mort aux Chats (Peter Porter)

prayer: 'Sometime during Eternity' (Lawrence Ferlinghetti)
'Pied Beauty' (G. M. Hopkins)
'Prayer before Birth' (Louis MacNeice)
'Cat and Mouse' (Ted Hughes)

people: 'Evans' (R. S. Thomas)
The Canterbury Tales: The General Prologue (Chaucer)
The Love-Song of J. Alfred Prufrock (T. S. Eliot)
'Miss Gee' (W. H. Auden)

war: 'An Irish Airman Foresees His Death' (W.B. Yeats)
'Base Details and The General' (Siegfried Sassoon)
'Your Attention Please' (Peter Porter)
Vergissmeinnicht (Keith Douglas)

It would add a wide dimension to the coursework if the thematic work were to be extended to include references to prose and drama as well as poetry. The danger here is that in attempting to cover several works, none of them is treated in any depth. Once again, it is a question of striking the balance between the various coursework options that are available. It should be clear from a moment's reflection, however, that it would be interesting and demanding to relate your reading of the poetry of Wilfred Owen to, for example, Robert Graves's memoir *Goodbye To All That* and R. C. Sherriff's play *Journey's End*. As your course develops, look for thematic links between the drama, poetry and prose that you are reading.

Coursework assignments on particular poems

As in the earlier section, all poems mentioned here can be found in the popular anthologies listed on pp.90–1.

1 Read two poems entitled 'Water', one by Ted Hughes, and one by Philip Larkin.

We usually take water for granted, thinking of it, if at all, as just another convenience. Consider the importance of water to life itself. Why, and of what, is it used as a symbol? What would you use it to symbolise? Imagine how you would feel about water if you lived in a more primitive, or non-industrial society; then how you would feel if you lived in a hot land. Write your own views on 'Water'.

2 Read 'Memories of Verdun' by Alan Dugan. Write a conversation between one of the 'sheep' and the poet on the subject of courage.

3 Read 'The Lovers' by W. R., Rodgers.

We all know what it is to be inwardly angry about something – the 'resentment' of the poem; this state can be short-lived, as in the poem, or may last for years. Imagine the moment when something makes you at last explode into anger, the relief with which you finally pour out your feelings, the 'outward and widening wave' of eloquence which your passion and conviction create. Choose any subject, but make sure it is something you feel strongly about, and for which you blame someone. Don't set the scene, just start . . .

4 'The Lodging-House Fuchsias'

Mrs Masters's fuchsias hung
Higher and broader, and brightly swung,
   Bell-like, more and more
Over the narrow garden path,
Giving the passer a sprinkle bath
   In the morning.

She put up with their pushful ways,
And made us tenderly lift their sprays,
   Going to her door:
But when her funeral had to pass
They cut back all the flowery mass
   In the morning.

Thomas Hardy

You have been bequeathed a valueless possession, much cherished by its previous owner, a relative/friend. Write a conversation between yourself and the solicitor, or between members of the deceased's family, in which the future of this object is decided.

5 'Symphony in Yellow'

An omnibus across the bridge
   Crawls like a yellow butterfly,
   And, here and there, a passer-by
Shows like a little restless midge.

Big barges full of yellow hay
   Are moored against the shadowy wharf,

  And like a yellow silken scarf,
The thick fog hangs along the quay.

The yellow leaves begin to fade
  And flutter from the Temple elms,
  And at my feet the pale green Thames
Lies like a rod of rippled jade.

Oscar Wilde

The poem above contains a number of similes (comparisons). Write a poem or a series of phrases or sentences in which you use similes in order to make your descriptions more vivid. Make sure that they contribute to the reader's understanding and enjoyment of what you have written.

  Examine the meaning of the word 'Symphony'. Why do you think the poet has used it here? In what ways is his poem like a musical composition? Write a short essay showing clearly why you think this poem might be compared to either (a) a piece of music or (b) a painting.

  Write a passage of description in which you use your two favourite colours as the main elements in the scene, room, place, etc., and try to create a particular atmosphere as you do so – of happiness, or fear, or of any other mood to which they are suited.

6 'The Clod and the Pebble'

'Love seeketh not itself to please,
Nor for itself hath any care;
But for another gives its ease,
And builds a Heaven in Hell's despair.'

So sung a little Clod of Clay
Trodden with the cattle's feet,
But a Pebble of the brook
Warbled out these metres meet:

'Love seeketh only Self to please,
To bind another to Its delight,
Joys in another's loss of ease,
And builds a Hell in Heaven's despite.'

William Blake

Write an appreciation of the sounds of the poem, and bring out clearly the poet's use of contrast. In what ways is the poem made the more effective by the use of dialogue?

Basing your answer on either the views of the Clod *or* the Pebble, write a passage (story or poem) which demonstrates either the selfishness or the unselfishness of love.

7 'The Blacksmiths'

Swart, swarthy smiths besmattered with smoke
Drive me to death with the din of their dints.
Such noise on nights heard no one never;
What knavish cry and clattering of knocks!
The snub-nosed changelings cry after 'Coal! Coal!'
And blow their bellows till all their brains burst:
'Huff, puff!' pants one; 'Haff, paff!' another.
They spit and sprawl and spin many yarns;
They grind teeth and gnash them and groan together,
Hot with the heaving of their hard hammers.
Aprons they have of hide of the bull.
Their shanks are shielded from the fierce sparks:
Heavy hammers they have, that are hard-handled;
Stark strokes they strike on an anvil of steel.
Lus, bus! Las, das! They strike in rotation:
The Devil destroy such a doleful din.
The master lengthens a little piece, belabours a smaller.
Twines the two together, and strikes a treble note
Tik, tak! Hic, hac! Tiket, taket! Tik, tak!
Lus, bus! Las, das! Such lives they lead
All horseshoers; Christ give them sorrow
For none for these water burners at night may rest.

Anonymous

What do you find unusual about this poem and what, if anything, do you find familiar about it?

In what ways do the sounds contribute to the effect of the poem? Refer to the text in some detail in order to bring out the actual noises which are being described.

Basing your ideas on the description and the atmosphere of the poem, write a passage (or a poem) in which various sounds (but not those used here) are used to create a particular effect. You might consider writing a scene in a car factory, or in some other branch of industry which you either know of or where there is an opportunity for you to exercise your imagination.

You will have noticed that there is an atmosphere of either nightmare or fear in the poem. Write two paragraphs (or more if you wish) in which the effect of noise or of particular sounds creates apprehension, worry or tension in the listener.

Some people cannot stand noise. Imagine that your car has broken down, and that you have to sit in it outside a noisy place which produces feelings of frustration or claustrophobia in you. Write an account of the experience, listing the particular sounds and the overall effect of the sounds on you.

This poem is all about sounds. Write a passage which contrasts completely with it by making the emphasis on silence and one's feelings during a period of silence.

8 'The Send-Off'

Down the close darkening lanes they sang their way
To the siding-shed,
And lined the train with faces grimly gay.

Their breasts were stuck all white with wreath and spray
As men's are, dead.

Dull porters watched them, and a casual tramp
Stood staring hard,
Sorry to miss them from the upland camp.

Then, unmoved, signals nodded, and a lamp
Winked to the guard.

So secretly, like wrongs hushed-up, they went.
They were not ours:
We never heard to which front these were sent;

Nor there if they yet mock what women meant
Who gave them flowers.

Shall they return to beating of great bells
In wild train-loads?
A few, a few, too few for drums and yells,

May creep back, silent, to village wells,
Up half-known roads.

Wilfred Owen

Compare this poem with 'Anthem for Doomed Youth' (p.68) indicating in what ways it is similar to that poem and in what ways it differs from it. You should write about the subject-matter and the verse form in which each poem is written.

The poem is set during the First World War. Imagine that you are one of those who is being given a send-off. Write two paragraphs indicating the nature of your feelings at the time *and* your feelings as you go to your unknown destination. You should base your writing on the mood of the poem. *OR* Imagine that you are one of those – friend or girlfriend or relative – who is at the send-off. In two paragraphs describe your feelings at the time and after your loved one has gone, again basing your writing on the mood of the poem.

Wilfred Owen once wrote about 'the pity of war'. What elements of pity is he directly concerned with in this poem?

9 'For Women'

To unpraise women it were a shame,
For a woman was thy dame;
Our blessed Lady bereth the name
Of all women wher that they go.

A woman is a worthy thing:
They do the washe and do the wringe;
'Lullay, lullay,' she doth thee singe,
And yet she hath but care and woo.

A woman is a worthy wight
She serveth man both daye and night,
Therto she putteth all her might,
And yet she hath but care and woo.

Anonymous (14th century)

Do you find 'For Women' a patronizing poem, written by a male chauvinist, or is it an early example of the move towards women's liberation? Write a modern lyric for a song on the same subject.

10 'London'

I wander thro' each charter'd street,
Near where the charter'd Thames does flow,
And mark in every face I meet
Marks of weakness, marks of woe.

In every cry of every Man,
In every Infant's cry of fear,
In every voice, in every ban,
The mind-forg'd manacles I hear.

How the Chimney-sweeper's cry
Every black'ning Church appalls;
And the hapless Soldier's sigh
Runs in blood down Palace walls.

But most thro' midnight streets I hear
How the youthful Harlot's curse
Blasts the new born Infant's tear,
And blights with plagues the Marriage hearse.

William Blake

Read through the poem carefully. Think about the images in the poem and say what picture they combine to give of London in the eighteenth century.

Using material in the poem, compare and contrast the statements made by the poet with any modern sufferings, at the same time indicating briefly where the differences lie between the eighteenth century and modern London.

Write a description of a modern city or town from your own standpoint, saying clearly what you find to criticize in its ways of life.

11 From Book I of *The Prelude* (1850)

One summer evening (led by her) I found
A little boat tied to a willow tree
Within a rocky cave, its usual home.
Straight I unloosed her chain, and stepping in
Pushed from the shore. It was an act of stealth
And troubled pleasure, nor without the voice
Of mountain-echoes did my boat move on;
Leaving behind her still, on either side,
Small circles glittering idly in the moon,
Until they melted all into one track
Of sparkling light. But now, like one who rows,
Proud of his skill, to reach a chosen point
With an unswerving line, I fixed my view
Upon the summit of a craggy ridge,
The horizon's utmost boundary; for above
Was nothing but the stars and the grey sky.
She was an elfin pinnace; lustily
I dipped my oars into the silent lake,
And, as I rose upon the stroke, my boat
Went heaving through the water like a swan;
When, from behind that craggy steep till then
The horizon's bound, a huge peak, black and huge,
As if with voluntary power instinct
Upreared its head. I struck and struck again,
And growing still in stature the grim shape
Towered up between me and the stars, and still,

For so it seemed, with purpose of its own
And measured motion like a living thing,
Strode after me. With trembling oars I turned,
And through the silent water stole my way
Back to the covert of the willow tree;
There in her mooring-place I left my bark, –
And through the meadows homeward went, in grave
And serious mood; but after I had seen
That spectacle, for many days, my brain
Worked with a dim and undetermined sense
Of unknown modes of being; o'er my thoughts
There hung a darkness, call it solitude
Or blank desertion. No familiar shapes
Remained, no pleasant images of trees,
Of sea or sky, no colours of green fields;
But huge and mighty forms, that do not live
Like living men, moved slowly through the mind
By day, and were a trouble to my dreams.

William Wordsworth

Read this part of an autobiographical poem by William Wordsworth. Give an account in your own words of the experience related here. Why is this incident fixed in the writer's mind?

Write an account of an experience in which you felt you were being watched. Using the autobiographical tone present in the extract above, try to create the atmosphere of secrecy and apprehension and particularly of adventure in your writing.

The poem conveys a solitary and unusual experience by night, in which physical description plays an important part. Bearing this in mind, write a description of a journey you have undertaken, making sure that you describe fully for your reader the kind of area or areas through which you passed.

12 'The Unquiet Grave'

'The wind doth blow today, my love,
  And a few small drops of rain;
I never had but one true-love;
  In cold grave she was lain.

'I'll do as much for my true-love
  As any young man may;
I'll sit and mourn all at her grave
  For a twelvemonth and a day.'

The twelvemonth and a day being up,
   The dead began to speak:
'Oh who sits weeping on my grave,
   And will not let me sleep?'

''Tis I, my love, sits on your grave.
   And will not let you sleep;
For I crave one kiss of your cold-clay lips,
   And that is all I seek.'

'You crave one kiss of my cold-clay lips;
   But my breath smells earthly strong;
If you have one kiss of my cold-clay lips,
   Your time will not be long.

''Tis down in yonder green garden,
   Love, where we used to walk,
The finest flower that ere was seen
   Is withered to a stalk.

'The stalk is withered dry, my love,
   So will our hearts decay;
So make yourself content, my love,
   Till God calls you away.'

Anonymous

'Is My Team Ploughing?'

'Is my team ploughing,
   That I used to drive
And hear the harness jingle
When I was man alive?'

Ay, the horses trample,
   The harness jingles now;
No change though you lie under
   The land you used to plough.

'Is football playing
   Along the river shore,
With lads to chase the leather,
   Now I stand up no more?'

Ay, the ball is flying,
   The lads play heart and soul;
The goal stands up, the keeper
   Stands up to keep the goal.

'Is my girl happy
   That I thought hard to leave,
And has she tired of weeping
   As she lies down at eve?'

Ay, she lies down lightly,
   She lies not down to weep;
Your girl is well contented.
   Be still, my lad, and sleep.

'Is my friend hearty,
   Now I am thin and pine,
And has he found to sleep in,
   A better bed than mine?'

Yes, lad, I lie easy,
   I lie as lads would choose;
I cheer a dead man's sweetheart,
   Never ask me whose.

A. E. Housman

Tell the stories of these two ballads. Each imagines a conversation between the living and the dead. In what ways are the poems similar, and in what ways do they differ from one another?

Imagine someone or yourself who is dead viewing a particular scene or activity which he/she used to enjoy when alive. Write two paragraphs (keeping the poems here in mind) in which the person comments on what is being done and considers how he/she used to do it.

Describe a visit to a graveyard. Take any name or names from a tombstone which appeal to you and write a brief imaginary biography of the person who is buried there.

Write a passage on the influence of particular things from your past on your present behaviour and attitudes.

Write about an activity, experience, etc. which you would dearly like to have again. Indicate what appealed to you about it and why.

Further reading

All the syllabuses for English and English Literature GCSE stress the importance of wide reading. Some of your coursework must provide evidence of this. The reading that you do will help you to understand and write about the work you are going to concentrate on. The frequency and breadth of the reading will prepare you for coursework which may have to be done in controlled conditions – like a traditional examination. This will sometimes require a response to writing which has been chosen because it is likely to be unfamiliar to you, and which therefore will give your examiner a good idea of what you have really understood for yourself of what you have read. Making use of the following list, on a regular basis, is an indispensable part of preparation for GCSE. The list reflects the recommendations of the examinations groups responsible for syllabuses.

The Rattle Bag ed. Seamus Heaney and Ted Hughes

This is a substantial anthology of poems from all cultures and all ages. The poems are presented in an arbitrary alphabetical order so that they may be discovered by the reader without any thematic or historical links being imposed by the editors. The collection is an excellent source book for the student who wishes to browse or to improvise assignments.

Iron, Honey, Gold ed. David Holbrook

This anthology is particularly strong in its selection of folk ballads and narrative poetry.

Touchstones ed. Benton and Benton

Any one of the five books in this series is a useful source of material linked in some way by subject, the writer's technique and style, or the tone of the poem. The arrangement of the anthology provides plenty of opportunity for thematic work, and the books contain suggestions for student's writing which will make useful additions to a coursework file.

A Choice of Poets ed. Hewett

Grouped by author, and arranged chronologically, the collection introduces important writers of the last two hundred years. There are biographical notes as well as notes on the individual poems. These last in particular can be used to structure coursework assignments because, as well as explaining and commenting on essential aspects of the poems, the notes ask pertinent questions that a sensitive reader must answer for himself.

Voices ed. Summerfield
The series of anthologies offers a wide selection of poetry and will be especially useful to students who are inspired by the unusual and by contemporary writing.

Poetry 1900–65 ed. George Macbeth
A representative collection of the poetry of the most important poets of the century. Biographical introductions open each section, and there is a brief commentary on each poem.

The Oxford Book of English Verse ed. Dame Helen Gardner
An anthology of the finest in English poetry, from the earliest poems written in the language to the twentieth century.

Relevant Brodie's Notes

A Man for All Seasons
Hobson's Choice
A Taste of Honey
Death of a Salesman
An Inspector Calls
Antony and Cleopatra
Hamlet
Julius Caesar
Macbeth
The Merchant of Venice
A Midsummer Night's Dream
Romeo and Juliet
Twelfth Night
Billy Liar
Selected Poems of Philip Larkin